# A READER'S DIGEST SONGBOOK

# Treasury of Great
# SHOW TUNES

Editor: William L. Simon
Music arranged and edited by Dan Fox
Senior Staff Editor: Mary Kelleher
Designer: Judy Speicher
Staff Editor: Richard Hessney
Editorial Assistant: Mark Pengelski
Annotations by Roy Hemming
Music Associate: Elizabeth Mead
Rights Manager: Lisa Garrett Smith
Music Typesetters: Irwin Rabinowitz and Saul Honigman

READER'S DIGEST GENERAL BOOKS
*Editor in Chief:* John A. Pope, Jr.
*Managing Editor:* Jane Polley
*Executive Editor:* Susan J. Wernert
*Art Director:* David Trooper
*Group Editors:* Will Bradbury, Sally French, Norman B. Mack, Kaari Ward
*Group Art Editors:* Evelyn Bauer, Robert M. Grant, Joel Musler
*Chief of Research:* Laurel A. Gilbride
*Copy Chief:* Edward W. Atkinson
*Picture Editor:* Richard Pasqual
*Rights and Permissions:* Pat Colomban
*Head Librarian:* Jo Manning

THE READER'S DIGEST ASSOCIATION, INC.
Pleasantville, New York/Montreal

ISBN 0-89577-495-X

# TREASURY OF GREAT SHOW TUNES

## INDEX TO SECTIONS

## INDEX TO SONGS

# INTRODUCTION

You won't find much argument among music historians about America's great show tunes being among the 20th century's most extraordinary and significant musical legacies. There's also little doubt as we approach the start of a new century that songs from *My Fair Lady, Show Boat, Anything Goes, South Pacific, Guys and Dolls* and many other Broadway classics will continue to flourish well into the 21st century—just as symphonic and operatic classics of previous eras have survived (and thrived) in the 20th.

What's more, it won't be merely through the recordings and videos of well-known singers and instrumentalists that these songs survive. Now, with songbooks such as this one, *all* show-tune lovers can get into the act—from bathtub baritones and shower-stall sopranos to parlor pianists and camp-fire guitarists.

You'll find that the word "treasury" in this collection's title is well chosen. There are 91 all-time gems by George and Ira Gershwin, Cole Porter, Jerome Kern, Harold Arlen, Rodgers and Hart, Rodgers and Hammerstein, Irving Berlin, Frank Loesser, Jule Styne, Kurt Weill, Leonard Bernstein, Cy Coleman, Jerry Herman and other American music greats. The songs come from the earliest revues of the pre-World War I years and continue right up to musicals of the 1990s. You may not always recognize the titles of the shows—*Garrick Gaieties, Show Girl, Rhythmania, Leave It to Me, Stop! Look! Listen!*—but you'll surely recognize the songs that came from them.

There are happy songs, sad songs, love songs, out-of-love songs, dramatic songs, novelty songs and all sorts of variations in between. Many were nightly showstoppers in their original productions. Some survived outright flops or musicals with limited Broadway runs and became durable hits on their own.

All of the tunes have been given wonderfully fresh and stylish new settings by Dan Fox, whose arrangements for our other music books have won him accolade after accolade from professional musicians and amateur hobbyists alike. His arrangements have no finger-busting virtuoso passages or way-out chords, yet they are not oversimplified either. They feature rich, colorful harmonies and, where appropriate, a vivid rhythmic flair. Most important: the melodic line remains first and foremost, inviting you to sing and play—and have a great time doing so.

As with our previous books, the selections have been compiled and edited by musician and musicologist Bill Simon. For many years Bill was senior music editor of the Reader Digest's Recorded Music Division, and he continues to be in charge of our songbook program. He also remains active as a performing musician, primarily in clubs in the New York City area.

The capsule introductions to the selections were written by cultural historian and critic Roy Hemming. Roy has been a principal show-music and classic-pop critic for *Stereo Review* since the early 1970s, and for several years he hosted a daily show-music program for radio station WAVZ in New Haven (scene of hundreds of pre-Broadway tryouts). He is also the author of *The Melody Lingers On: The Great Songwriters and Their Movie Musicals* and co-author (with David Hajdu) of *Discovering Great Singers of Classic Pop.*

—The Editors

## How to Use This Book

The arrangements in *Treasury of Great Show Tunes* were designed to be easy to play while remaining musically interesting and artistically gratifying. For players of any treble clef instrument, the melody is on top, clear and uncluttered, with the stems of the notes turned up. However, if one is to play in tandem with a piano or organ, it must be on a "C" instrument, such as a violin, flute, recorder, oboe, accordion, harmonica, melodica or electronic keyboard. Guitarists can also play the melody as written, or they can play chords from the symbols (G7, Am, etc.) or from the diagrams printed just above the staves. Organists whose instruments have foot pedals may use the *small* pedal notes in the bass clef (with stems turned down.) But *these pedal notes should not be attempted by pianists; they are for feet only!* For the sake of facility, the pedal lines move stepwise and stay within an octave. Players who improvise in the jazz sense can "take off" from the melody and the chord symbols.

The chord symbols also are designed for pianists who have studied the popular chord method; players can read the melody line and improvise their own left-hand accompaniments. The chord symbols may be used, too, by bass players (string or brass); just play the root note of each chord symbol, except where another note is indicated (for example, "D/F# bass"). Accordionists can use the chord symbols for the left-hand buttons while playing the treble portions of the arrangement as written.

**A note:** Many more great show tunes are included in the 14 other music books published by Reader's Digest. The books are *Family Songbook, Family Songbook of Faith and Joy, Festival of Popular Songs, Great Music's Greatest Hits, The Merry Christmas Songbook, Popular Songs That Will Live Forever, Country and Western Songbook, Unforgettable Musical Memories, Children's Songbook, Remembering Yesterday's Hits, Popular Classics, Parade of Popular Hits, The Easy Way to Play 100 Unforgettable Hits* and *Remembering the '50s.* (Songs may appear in more than one book, but the musical arrangements are always different.) You can order the books from Reader's Digest, Pleasantville, New York 10570.

*Illustration Credits:* Sheet music and decorative graphics from the collections of Frank Driggs, Linda Patterson Eger, James Merillat, William L. Simon, the Museum of the City of New York Theater Collection and another private collection.

Special permission granted from producers and organizations to reproduce show posters and logos on the following pages: pp. 82, 88, 95: The Rodgers and Hammerstein Theater Library; p. 136: Harry Rigby/Pyxidium Ltd.; p. 199: Angel and Capitol Records; pp. 212, 242: Cy Feuer and Ernest Martin; p. 222: George Abbott in association with Robert Fryer; p. 230: Harold Prince; p. 234: Cy Feuer and Ernest Martin in association with Frank Productions, Inc.; p. 237: Michael Kidd and N. Richard Nash; p. 240: David Merrick in association with Bernard Delfont; p. 246, 258: Fryer, Carr and Harris; p. 252: Alexander H. Cohen; p. 255: Lore Noto in association with Sheldon Baron and Dorothy Olim; p. 262: Ray Stark in association with Seven Arts Productions; p. 270: Mike Nichols and Associates; p. 277: Allan Carr and Associates; pp. 280, 286: New York Shakespeare Festival; Joseph Papp, Producer; p. 283: David Merrick.

# AUTUMN IN NEW YORK

Vernon Duke wrote "Autumn in New York" in 1934 as a follow-up to "April in Paris," which he and lyricist E. Y. (Yip) Harburg had contributed to the 1932 revue *Walk a Little Faster*. This time, Duke wrote both the music and lyrics himself — for a production number that was performed as the big finale of another revue, *Thumbs Up*, against two giant representations of the Manhattan skyline. The song came into its own as a pop standard in the 1940s, through recordings by Frank Sinatra, Jo Stafford and Billie Holiday, among others.

**from *Thumbs Up***    Words and Music by Vernon Duke

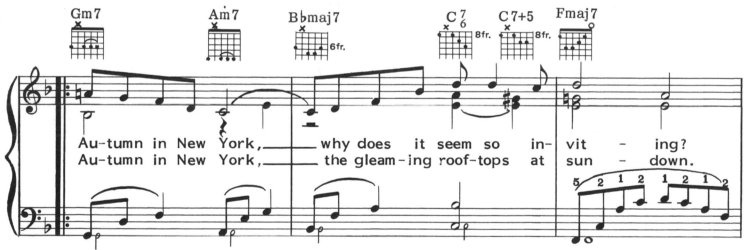

Au-tumn in New York, why does it seem so in-vit - ing?
Au-tumn in New York, the gleam-ing roof-tops at sun - down.

Au-tumn in New York, it spells the thrill of first-
Au-tumn in New York, it lifts you up when you're

# TIME ON MY HANDS

**from *Smiles***

The 1930 show *Smiles* had all the earmarks of a hit, with Florenz Ziegfeld as producer, a score by Vincent Youmans and stars such as Marilyn Miller and Fred and Adele Astaire. But it flopped. Moreover, "Time on My Hands" was dropped from the musical because Marilyn Miller didn't like singing it! An irate Youmans had the song published anyway, and it quickly became a hit.

Words by Harold Adamson and Mack Gordon; Music by Vincent Youmans

# HOW ARE THINGS IN GLOCCA MORRA?

Lyricist Yip Harburg seems to have had a way of making us believe unquestioningly in never-never lands. Eight years after he and Harold Arlen first transported us to the wonderful land of Oz (along with Judy Garland and friends, of course), Harburg had us dreaming about the mythical Irish village of Glocca Morra, thanks to this now-classic ballad from *Finian's Rainbow*. Ella Logan introduced us to Glocca Morra's cheerful birds, leaping brooks and weeping willows in the long-running Broadway show, which opened in 1947. And Petula Clark sang the song in Francis Ford Coppola's 1968 movie version.

**from *Finian's Rainbow***

Words by E.Y. Harburg; Music by Burton Lane

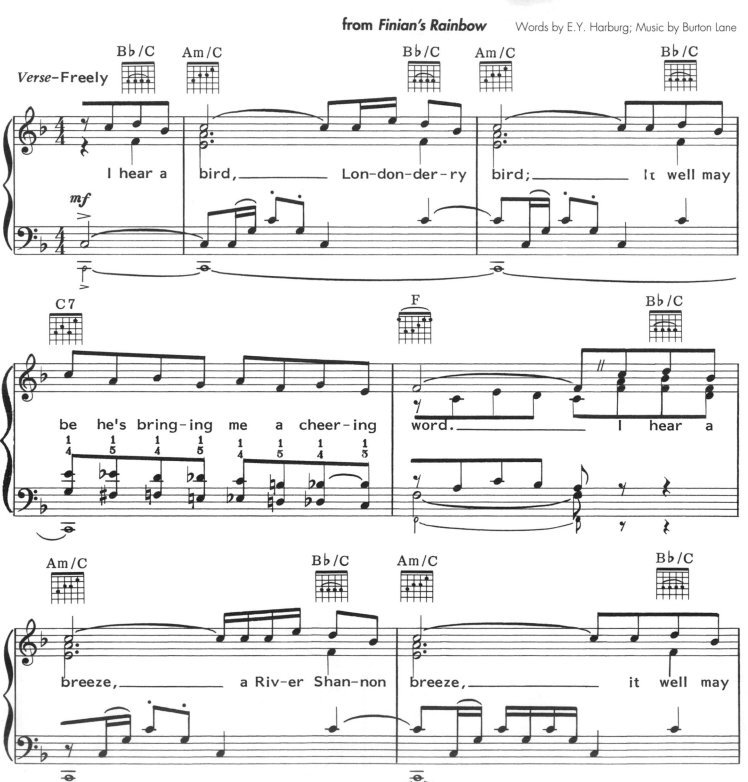

I hear a bird, Lon-don-der-ry bird; It well may be he's bring-ing me a cheer-ing word. I hear a breeze, a Riv-er Shan-non breeze, it well may

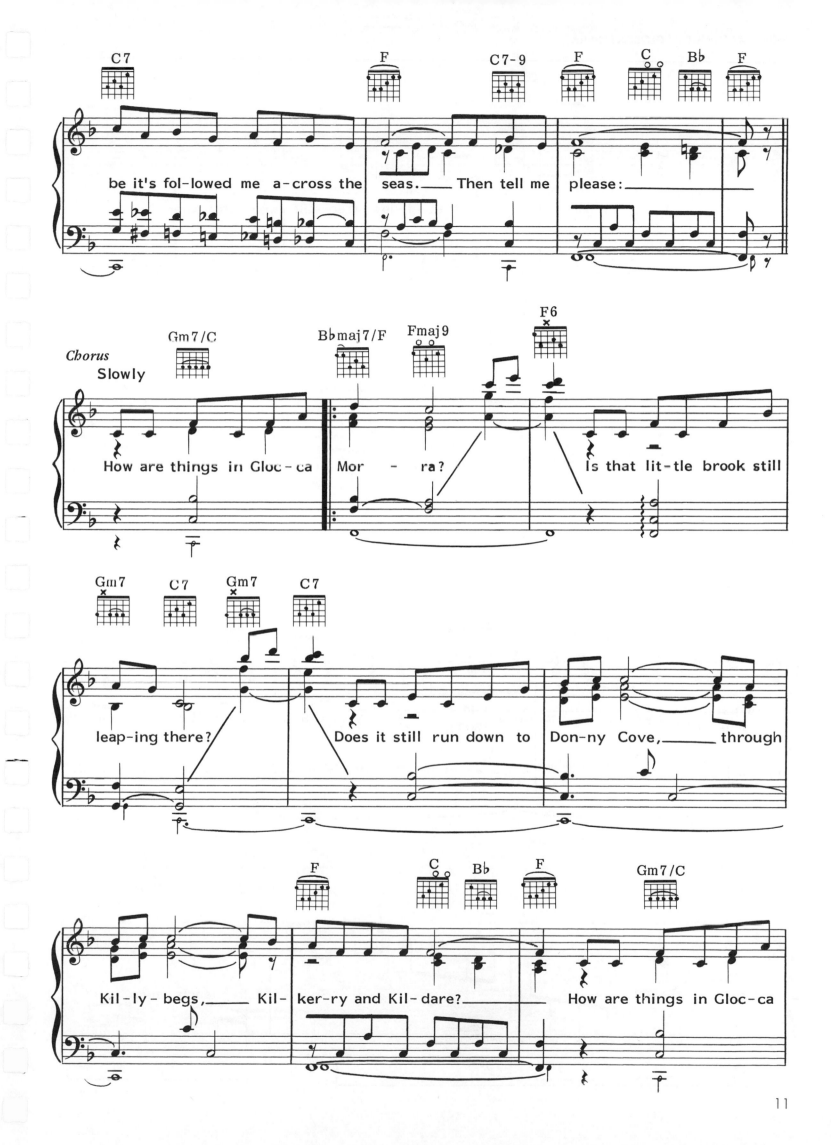

wil - low, and each brook a - long the way, and each

lad that comes a - whist - lin' too - ra -
lass that comes a - sigh - in' lay:___

slower, like a harp

How are things in Gloc - ca Mor - ra this fine

**1.** day?___ How are things in Gloc - ca

**2.** slowing day?___

*8va lower*

13

# BUCKLE DOWN, WINSOCKI

Musical comedies set on college campuses were a Broadway and Hollywood staple of the 1920s and '30s. They usually involved unrealistic, cliché-filled variations of the "big game" plot, mixed in with various romantic rivalries — but they also featured youthful performers bursting with vim, vigor and talent. When *Best Foot Forward* opened in 1941, it had plenty of all that, plus enough fresh, tongue-in-cheek touches to keep audiences rooting for the boys from the fictional Winsocki prep school located somewhere near Philadelphia. Their rousing rallying cry, "Buckle Down, Winsocki," has endured as one of the warmest memories of the glory days of the collegiate musical.

from *Best Foot Forward*

Words by Ralph Blane; Music by Hugh Martin

14

make them wrecks, you can break the hex, so buck - le
on the chin, you are bound to win, if you will

**1.** down!_____ Make 'em

**2.** on - ly buck - le down. If you

fight, you'll chuck - le at de - feat._____ If you

fight, your luck - 'll not re - treat._____

(Shout) We repeat: Knuck - le

15

**BUCKLE DOWN, WINSOCKI**

*\* Go back to the introduction at the very beginning.*

# BY MYSELF

There aren't many songs that might be called paeans to self-sufficiency — or that take such an assertive, nonpitying view of the end of romance as this one. Overshadowed by the Dietz and Schwartz ballad "I See Your Face Before Me" during the three-month run of *Between the Devil* in 1937, "By Myself" became a standard after it was polished up by Fred Astaire for the 1953 movie *The Band Wagon*. Judy Garland and Peggy Lee are among the many other singers whose recordings helped turn it into a pop classic.

**from *Between the Devil***    Words by Howard Dietz; Music by Arthur Schwartz

**BY MYSELF**

*Chorus*—with a relaxed feeling

# DANCING IN THE DARK

With its fatalistic lyrics by Howard Dietz, this is one of the darkest songs ever to become a superhit. The lyricist even had doubts about using the song in the 1931 revue for which it was written, *The Band Wagon*, starring Fred and Adele Astaire. But Arthur Schwartz's melody is so memorably appealing that the words never seem as forlorn as they might otherwise. Without lyrics, the song became one of the most romantic of all movie *pas de deux*— danced by Fred Astaire and Cyd Charisse in the 1953 film *The Band Wagon* (which bore no relationship to the original Broadway revue, except for Astaire and some of the score).

from *The Band Wagon*   Words by Howard Dietz; Music by Arthur Schwartz

# WHAT IS THERE TO SAY

Vernon Duke fled his native Russia as a teenager in the aftermath of the Bolshevik revolution, and at first composed classical scores under his real name, Vladimir Dukelsky. But he also developed a love for popular music and, as Vernon Duke, began writing for the musical theater. On settling permanently in the United States in 1929, he became friends with Yip Harburg and Ira Gershwin and began collaborating with them on songs for Broadway shows. He wrote "What Is There to Say?" for the first *Ziegfeld Follies* to be produced under the name of Ziegfeld's debt-ridden widow after the legendary showman's death.

**from *Ziegfeld Follies of 1934***     Words by E.Y. Harburg; Music by Vernon Duke

What is there to say? And what is there to do? The dream I've been seek-ing has prac-tic-'ly speak-ing come true.

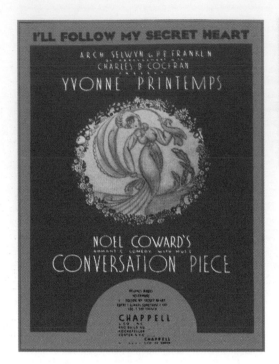

# I'LL FOLLOW MY SECRET HEART

Hard times often unleash nostalgic looks back to earlier and presumably happier eras—and so the Great Depression of the 1930s brought to Broadway *The Great Waltz* (with a score based on the melodies of the Johann Strausses, Sr. and Jr.) and Noel Coward's 1936 London hit *Conversation Piece*. Coward's romantic tale of Regency England had wit, elegance, charm and the vivaciously kinetic French operetta star Yvonne Printemps. The show lasted only 55 performances, but "I'll Follow My Secret Heart" lasted longer on the music charts, rising into the Top Ten, thanks mainly to Ray Noble's dance-band recording.

**from *Conversation Piece***          Words and Music by Noel Coward

27

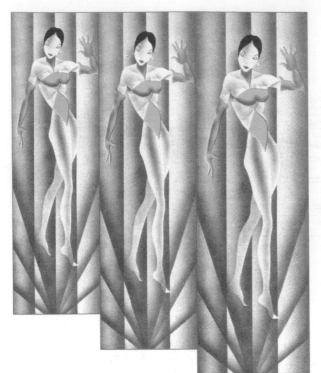

# I LIKE THE LIKES OF YOU

Yip Harburg's way with words first blossomed on New York's Lower East Side, where he and classmate Ira Gershwin wrote poems for their high-school paper. When the 1929 stock-market crash short-circuited the electrical appliance business that Harburg had started after college, Ira put him in touch with composers with whom he began writing lyrics for Broadway revues. It wasn't long before Harburg became known as one of the era's most skillful and inventive lyricists — and remained so for the next five decades. His and Vernon Duke's "I Like the Likes of You" was introduced in the '34 *Ziegfeld Follies* by Judith Barron and Brice Hutchins, who later became famous under his real name, Bob Cummings.

**from *Ziegfeld Follies of 1934***      Words by E.Y. Harburg; Music by Vernon Duke

* smaller bands can play:

# Rhode Island Is Famous for You

**Inside U.S.A.**
*A MUSICAL REVUE*

In 1948, Arthur Schwartz came up with the idea of reversing the theme of the around-the-world 1935 revue *At Home Abroad* (for which he and Howard Dietz had written the score) by focusing on a cross-country "tour" of the United States. For it, he secured rights to the title of John Gunther's best-selling book *Inside U.S.A.* The show's big song was the torchy "Haunted Heart." But just as durable has been "Rhode Island Is Famous for You"—in which Dietz and Schwartz offer a wildly sly and outrageously punning inventory of various states and what they are famous for.

**from *Inside U.S.A.***     Words by Howard Dietz; Music by Arthur Schwartz

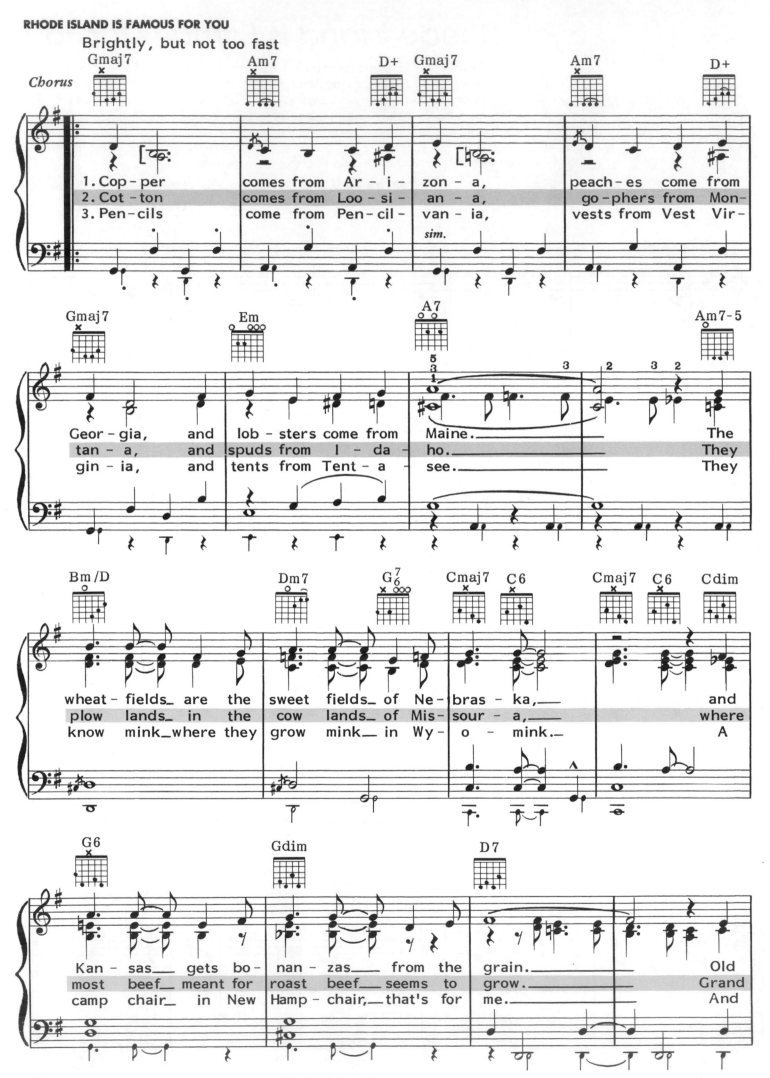

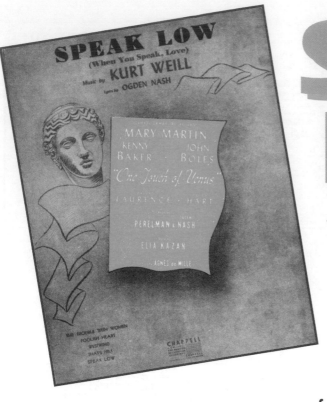

# SPEAK LOW

Kurt Weill, of course, had won international fame in the late 1920s, collaborating in his native Germany with Bertolt Brecht on such works as *The Three-Penny Opera* and *Mahagonny*. Eventually, after fleeing the Nazis, he came to America. *One Touch of Venus* was originally created for another German expatriate, Marlene Dietrich. But when she decided against giving Broadway a try, Mary Martin took over (it was her first starring role on the Great White Way). Night after night, she stopped the show with this haunting romantic ballad, which quickly made it to *Your Hit Parade*.

**from *One Touch of Venus***     Words by Ogden Nash; Music by Kurt Weill

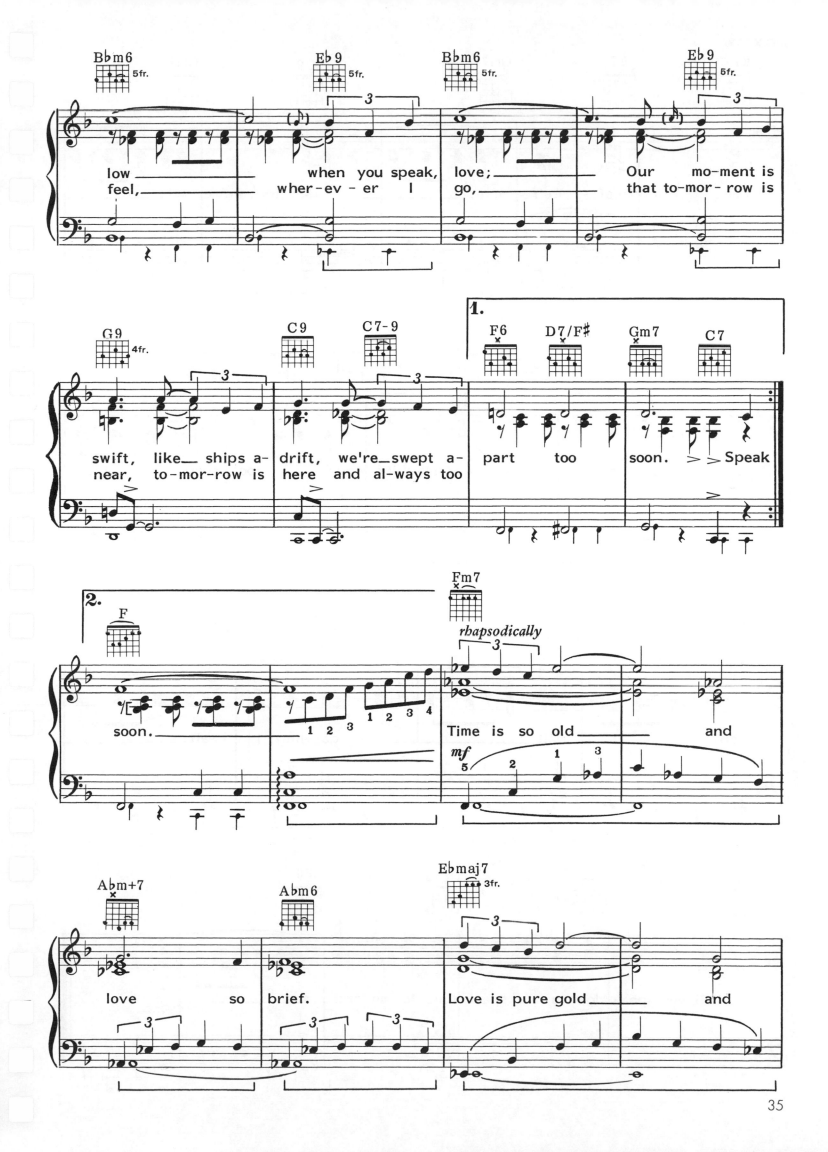

Lady in the Dark, with a cast headed by Gertrude Lawrence and Danny Kaye, made Broadway history in 1941: it was the first musical to deal seriously — although perhaps none too realistically — with the subject of psychoanalysis. A fragment of "My Ship" is used as a recurring theme throughout the play. Finally, in the last act, the song is heard in its entirety for the first time — and it serves to release the heroine's mental block. When the movie version of Lady in the Dark was made in 1944, "My Ship" (along with about 90 percent of the Weill-Gershwin score) was dropped. The song has long since survived Hollywood's miscalculations and become an enduring standard.

**from Lady in the Dark**   Words by Ira Gershwin; Music by Kurt Weill

My ship has sails that are made of silk, the decks are trimmed with gold, and of jam and spice there's a par-a-dise in the hold. My ship's a-glow with a

# LET'S PUT OUT THE LIGHTS AND GO TO SLEEP

Rudy Vallee was a big booster of Herman Hupfeld's songs, being the first to record "As Time Goes By" and "When Yuba Plays the Rhumba on the Tuba (down in Cuba)" in 1931. The following year, Vallee was all set to sing "Let's Put Out the Lights and Go to Bed," just introduced in *George White's Music Hall Varieties*, on his radio show—when NBC's censors insisted that the word "bed" be eliminated. With only minutes to spare before air time, the singer suggested changing "bed" to "sleep." Shortly afterward Vallee recorded the song in its original version. But Hupfeld, to forestall further broadcasting problems, agreed to publish it as "...and Go to Sleep," and it became a major hit in that form.

**from *George White's Music Hall Varieties***      Words and Music by Herman Hupfeld

\* The *Schottische* dance came out of Scotland in the mid-19th century. Its light, skipping rhythm suggests a *polka*, slowed down. Think of Lawrence Welk's "Champagne Music."

drink; Leave those dish-es in the sink; What's to do a-bout it? Sim-ply night-y night and so to sleep. You're wait-ing now for me to say: "I love you more and more and more, dear. You're look-ing young-er ev - 'ry day.

# APRIL · IN · PARIS

Is there a romantic soul anywhere who hasn't dreamed of spending springtime in Paris . . . especially after hearing "April in Paris"? Vernon Duke credited actor Monty Woolley with the idea, as part of the 1932 revue *Walk a Little Faster*, which Woolley directed. The critics had generally good things to say about the show's star, Beatrice Lillie, but not much about the song or Evelyn Hoey, who introduced it. Nonetheless, dance bands picked up the tune, and within a short time *Variety* was listing it among the nation's Top Ten. It has remained a pop standard ever since, and even provided Doris Day with the title song for one of her most popular '50s movie musicals.

**Rather freely**

**from *Walk a Little Faster***

Words by E.Y. Harburg; Music by Vernon Duke

## THE RODGERS AND HART SHOWS

# THERE'S A SMALL HOTEL

Few songwriters were ever less alike than Richard Rodgers (who could have passed for a conservative banker) and Larry Hart (the undisciplined, puckish "eternal sophomore," as one biographer called him). Yet together they wrote songs that endure among Broadway's greatest creations for their blend of inventive melody and sophisticated verbal wit. The pair wrote this unabashedly romantic ballad in 1935 as part of their score for Billy Rose's circus musical, *Jumbo*. But the song was cut just before the opening. A year later they worked it into *On Your Toes*, and it became that show's big hit (bigger, in fact, than any of *Jumbo*'s tunes).

**from *On Your Toes***          Words by Lorenz Hart; Music by Richard Rodgers

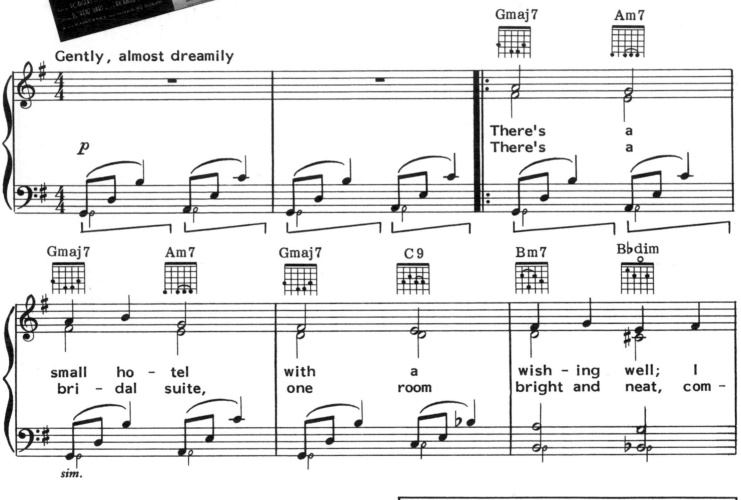

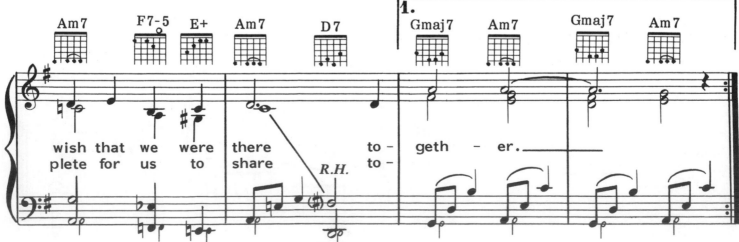

When *Pal Joey* opened in 1940, there had never been a musical quite like it—with its seamy, cynical John O'Hara story about a young nightclub hustler (Gene Kelly) and the rich, married, older woman (Vivienne Segal) he's entangled with. Although it sounds like a sincere love song, "I Could Write a Book" is merely part of a line that Joey (who, as Richard Rodgers said, "had probably never read a book in his life") hands a naive young girl. Over the years, many singers have been perfectly willing to take the lyrics at face value and have turned "I Could Write a Book" into one of Rodgers and Hart's most popular romantic standards.

# I COULD WRITE A BOOK

**from *Pal Joey***

Words by Lorenz Hart; Music by Richard Rodgers

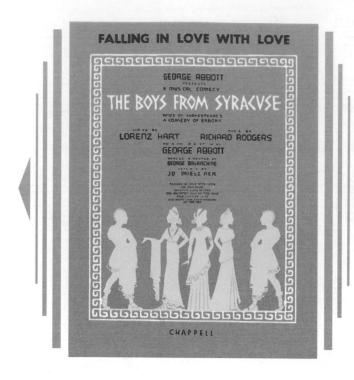

# FALLING IN LOVE WITH LOVE

Next to Irving Berlin, Richard Rodgers probably wrote more great popular tunes in three-quarter time than anyone outside of Vienna's famous Strauss family. Funny thing, though: people generally don't think of most of Rodgers' waltzes *as* waltzes. "Falling in Love with Love" is a good example. Its immediately hummable melody doesn't call attention to its gentle waltz beat, yet the sly lilt behind that beat helps mute the underlying cynicism of Hart's lyric about the undependability of love. In *The Boys from Syracuse*, the song is a lament for two of the show's love-hurt leading ladies. Later, of course, the script works out a happy ending for everybody.

**from *The Boys* from *Syracuse***  Words by Lorenz Hart; Music by Richard Rodgers

# THIS CAN'T BE LOVE

Lorenz Hart's lyrics for the romantic ballads he wrote with Richard Rodgers run the gamut from charmingly innocent to desperately self-pitying. Yet he wrote few more cheerfully sardonic stanzas than those for "This Can't Be Love." *The Boys from Syracuse*, based loosely on Shakespeare's *Comedy of Errors*, recounts the romantic misadventures of two sets of twins in ancient Greece. The 1940 movie version replaced most of the ribald wit of the show with broader comedy hijinks and anachronistic visual gags (such as trolley-car chariots). It also kept only four of the Broadway songs, this one (fortunately) among them.

from *The Boys from Syracuse*    Words by Lorenz Hart; Music by Richard Rodgers

This can't be love be-cause I feel so well; ___ No sobs, no sor-rows,___ no sighs. ___

Love, according to thousands of song lyrics, can have many strange effects on those smitten by it. For two of the young collegiate sweethearts in 1939's *Too Many Girls*, Larry Hart portrays love as completely discombobulating their sense of time. That idea (along with Richard Rodgers' beguiling melody, of course) obviously hit a responsive chord in millions of listeners, who promptly put "I Didn't Know What Time It Was" on *Your Hit Parade* for seven weeks—and have kept it a popular standard ever since. Marcy Westcott and Richard Kollmar introduced the song on Broadway, and Lucille Ball (dubbed by Trudi Erwin) sang it in the 1940 movie version.

# I DIDN'T KNOW WHAT TIME IT WAS

**from *Too Many Girls***    Words by Lorenz Hart; Music by Richard Rodgers

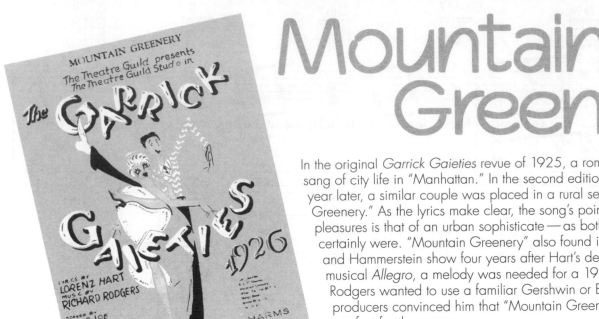

# Mountain Greenery

In the original *Garrick Gaieties* revue of 1925, a romantic young couple sang of city life in "Manhattan." In the second edition of the *Gaieties* a year later, a similar couple was placed in a rural setting to sing "Mountain Greenery." As the lyrics make clear, the song's point of view about rustic pleasures is that of an urban sophisticate—as both Rodgers and Hart certainly were. "Mountain Greenery" also found its way into a Rodgers and Hammerstein show four years after Hart's death. In the 1947 musical *Allegro*, a melody was needed for a 1920s prom sequence. Rodgers wanted to use a familiar Gershwin or Berlin tune, but the producers convinced him that "Mountain Greenery" would be perfect for the scene.

**from *The Garrick Gaieties***          Words by Lorenz Hart; Music by Richard Rodgers

63

# SPRING IS HERE

Rodgers and Hart wrote two different songs called "Spring Is Here," for two different musical comedies. The first one was written in 1929 for the modestly successful musical of the same name, and was forgotten as soon as the show closed. The second, more wistful "Spring Is Here" came nine years later for the much more successful *I Married an Angel*, starring dancer Vera Zorina. This "Spring" got another big boost when Jeanette MacDonald and Nelson Eddy sang it in the 1942 movie version of *I Married an Angel*, even though the film (with good reason) remains among the least-praised of the MacDonald-Eddy musicals.

**from *I Married an Angel***

Words by Lorenz Hart; Music by Richard Rodgers

Once there was a thing called spring when the world was writ-ing vers-es like
All the lads and girls would sing when we sat at lit-tle ta-bles and

yours and mine.

drank May wine.

Now A-pril, May and June are sad-ly out of tune. Life has stuck the pin in the bal-loon.

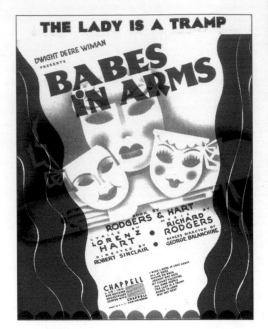

# THE LADY IS A TRAMP

In this spunky tribute to a nonconformist female, Larry Hart's ironic lyrics enumerate the various ways in which the lady of the title refuses to follow the conventions of "fashionable" folk. As a result, she may be a social outcast—a tramp—among her "betters," but she's proud of it. A teenaged Mitzi Green introduced "The Lady Is a Tramp" in Broadway's *Babes in Arms* in 1937. But when the movie version was filmed in 1939, MGM decided the song was inappropriate for another teenager, Judy Garland, and relegated it to instrumental background music. Nine years later, however, the studio permitted Lena Horne to let loose with a saucy rendition in its Rodgers and Hart "bio-pic," *Words and Music*.

**from *Babes in Arms***          Words by Lorenz Hart; Music by Richard Rodgers

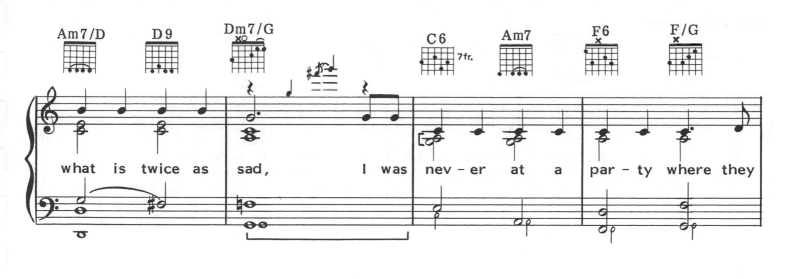

what is twice as sad, I was nev-er at a par-ty where they

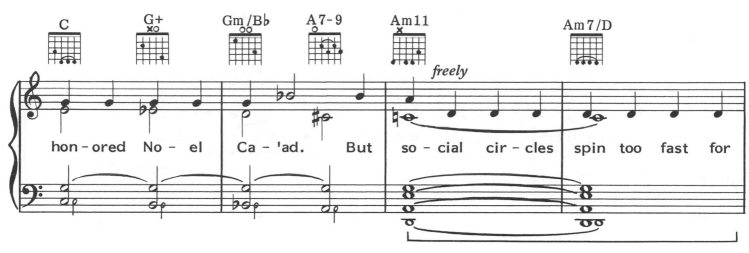

hon-ored No-el Ca-'ad. But so-cial cir-cles spin too fast for

me;_____ My Ho-bo-hem-ia is the place to

**Light and swingy** ($\sqcap$ = $\sqcap^3\sqcap$)

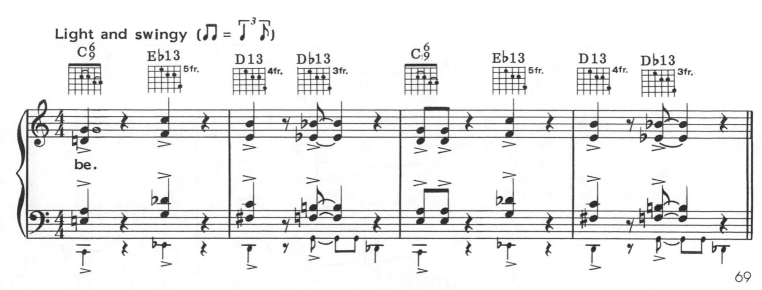

be.

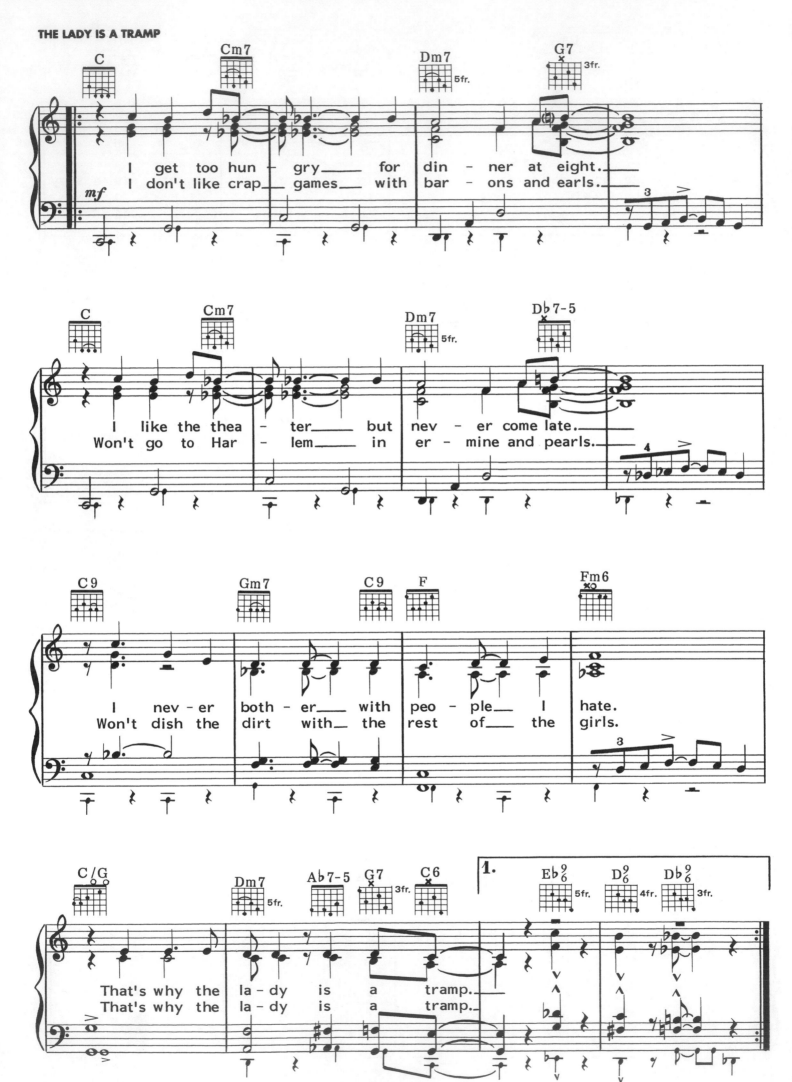

I get too hun - gry____ for din - ner at eight.____
I don't like crap____ games____ with bar - ons and earls.____

I like the thea - ter____ but nev - er come late.____
Won't go to Har - lem____ in er - mine and pearls.____

I nev - er both - er____ with peo - ple I hate.
Won't dish the dirt with____ the rest of____ the girls.

That's why the la - dy is a tramp.____
That's why the la - dy is a tramp.____

70

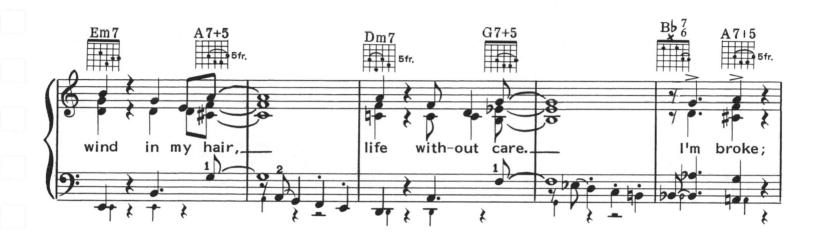

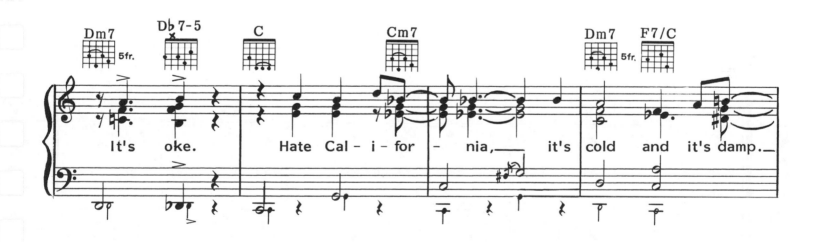

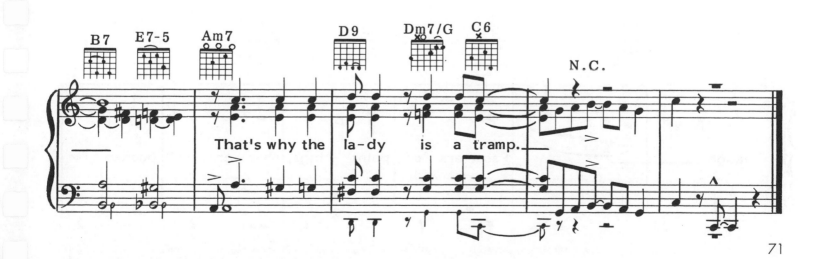

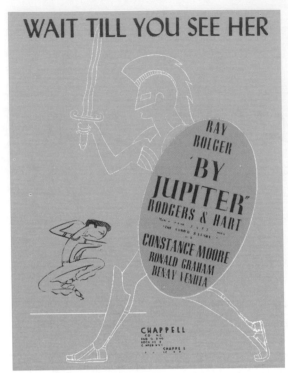

# WAIT TILL YOU SEE HER

Rodgers and Hart's longest-running Broadway musical (during its original run, that is) turned out to be their last: 1942's *By Jupiter*. The show poked fun at the age-old battle of the sexes — through its tale of ancient Greek warriors who invade a mythological Amazon kingdom ruled by women and get more than they bargain for. Rodgers (as co-producer as well as composer), faced with a show that was continually running late, decided to cut "Wait Till You See Her." Nonetheless, the song became a favorite of singers and orchestras, and Rodgers restored it to the show before the end of the run. (For the record, later Broadway revivals of *Pal Joey* and *The Boys from Syracuse* eventually outran *By Jupiter*.)

**from By Jupiter**     *Words by Lorenz Hart; Music by Richard Rodgers*

# HAVE YOU MET MISS JONES?

Except for this ballad, *I'd Rather Be Right* (1937) is better remembered as a George M. Cohan show than as a Rodgers and Hart creation. The ol' Yankee Doodle Dandy didn't get on well with the younger songwriters, and didn't hesitate to change their lyrics — despite their protests. The show was essentially a satiric revue with a thin story line about two young lovers who, in a dream, encounter President Franklin D. Roosevelt (played by Cohan). Most of the songs had a strictly '30s topical slant that has not helped their longevity. "Have You Met Miss Jones?" is another matter. The romantic remembrance of the two lovers' first meeting remains a favorite to the present day.

**from *I'd Rather Be Right***

Words by Lorenz Hart; Music by Richard Rodgers

# MANHATTAN

This musical accounting of some of the everyday attractions of their beloved hometown (the subway, the zoo, Central Park, Fifth Avenue, Mott Street, Greenwich Village, etc.) was originally intended for an early '20s Rodgers and Hart musical that was never produced (*Winkle Town*). In 1925 the songwriters added the song to a fund-raising revue that the Theatre Guild planned for two Sunday-evening performances at New York's Garrick Theater. When *The Garrick Gaieties* opened in May of 1925, "Manhattan" was the hit of the show. It became so popular that the Theatre Guild kept expanding the revue's engagement. The song has been among the team's most popular ever since.

**from *The Garrick Gaieties***

Words by Lorenz Hart; Music by Richard Rodgers

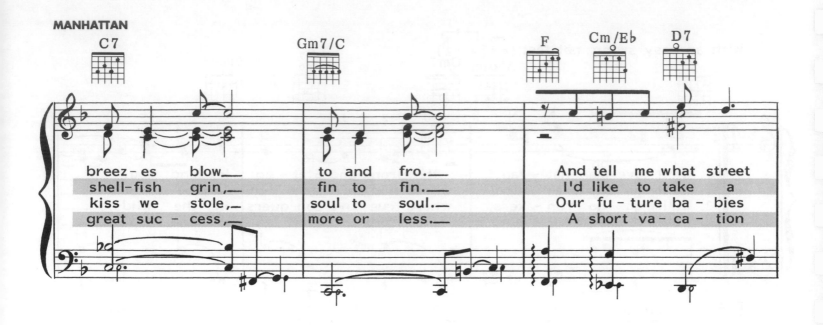

breez-es blow___ to and fro.___ And tell me what street
shell-fish grin,___ fin to fin.___ I'd like to take a
kiss we stole,___ soul to soul.___ Our fu-ture ba-bies
great suc-cess,___ more or less.___ A short va-ca-tion

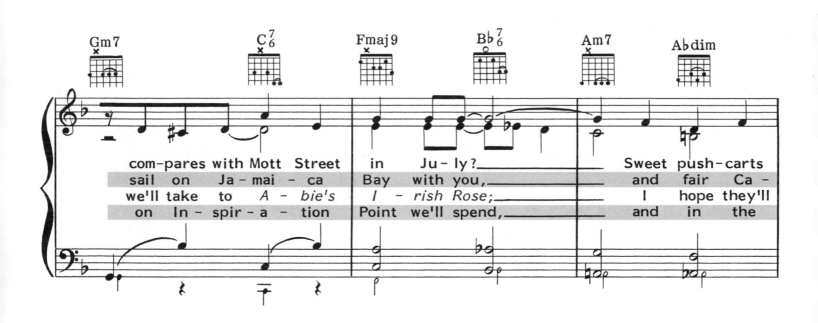

com-pares with Mott Street in Ju-ly?___ Sweet push-carts
sail on Ja-mai-ca Bay with you,___ and fair Ca-
we'll take to *A - bie's* *I - rish Rose;*___ I hope they'll
on In - spir - a - tion Point we'll spend,___ and in the

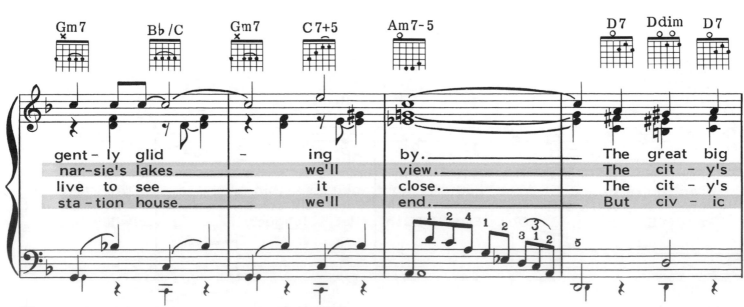

gent-ly glid - ing by.___ The great big
nar-sie's lakes___ we'll view.___ The cit - y's
live to see___ it close.___ The cit - y's
sta-tion house___ we'll end.___ But civ - ic

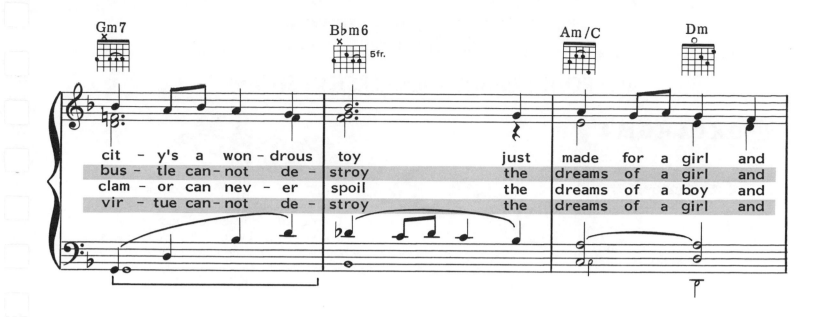

cit – y's a won – drous toy just made for a girl and
bus – tle can – not de – stroy the dreams of a girl and
clam – or can nev – er spoil the dreams of a boy and
vir – tue can – not de – stroy the dreams of a girl and

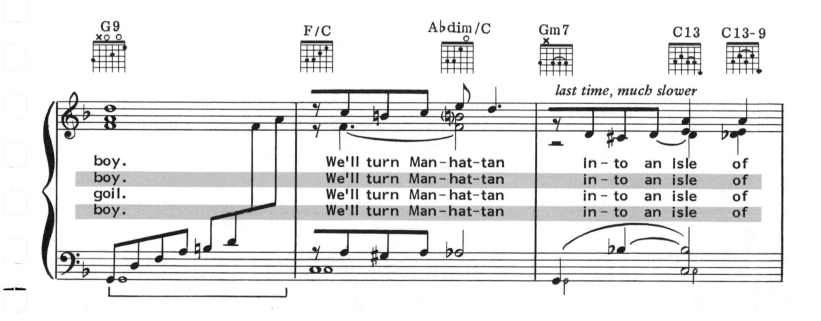

*last time, much slower*

boy. We'll turn Man–hat–tan in – to an isle of
boy. We'll turn Man–hat–tan in – to an isle of
goil. We'll turn Man–hat–tan in – to an isle of
boy. We'll turn Man–hat–tan in – to an isle of

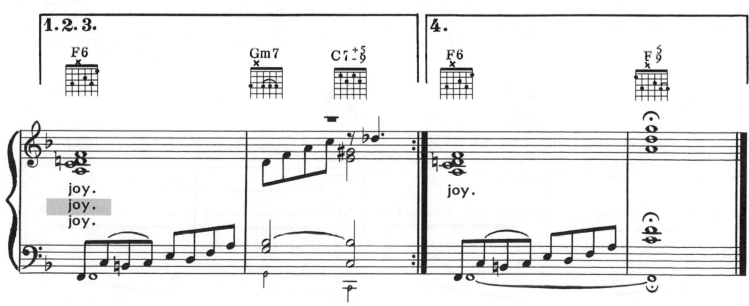

**1. 2. 3.**

joy.
joy.
joy.

**4.**

joy.

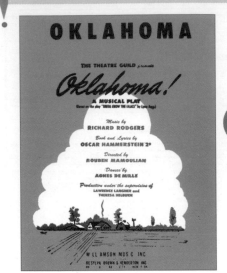

# OKLAHOMA

When Rodgers and Hammerstein's landmark musical *Oklahoma!* began its pre-Broadway tryout in New Haven as *Away We Go!*, this title tune was a solo for the cowboy hero. By opening night on Broadway— March 31, 1943 — it had become the show's rousing finale, featuring the entire company. What Rodgers and Hammerstein didn't know was that, six years earlier, Jimmy McHugh and Harold Adamson had written a song called "Oh, Oh, Oklahoma" (ending "Oklahoma, you're OK! Yip-ee-i-ay!") for a quickly forgotten Alice Faye movie, *You're a Sweetheart*. Both sets of songwriters later agreed it was another example of creative minds working separately and coming up with remarkably similar results.

**from *Oklahoma!***     Words by Oscar Hammerstein II; Music by Richard Rodgers

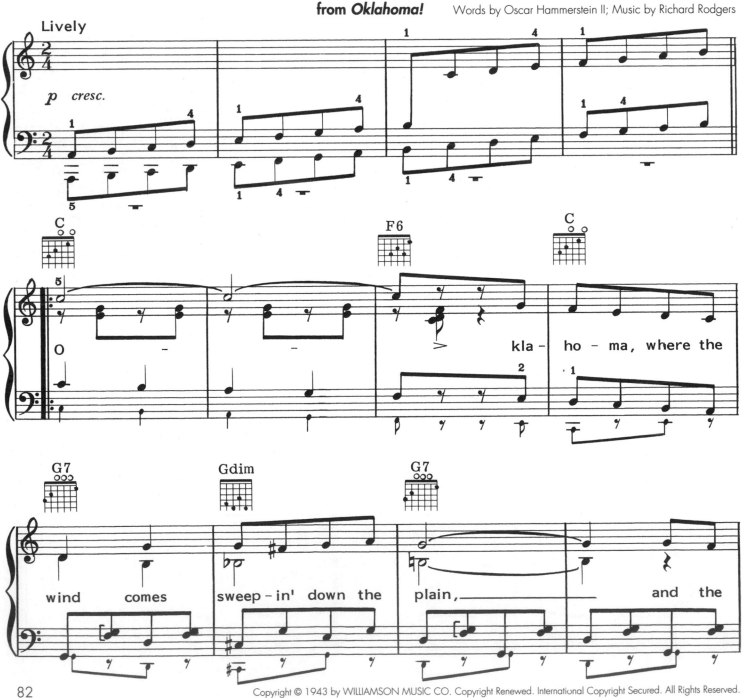

wav – in' wheat can sure smell sweet when the

wind comes right be – hind the rain.

O – – kla – ho – ma, ev – 'ry

night my hon – ey lamb and I sit a –

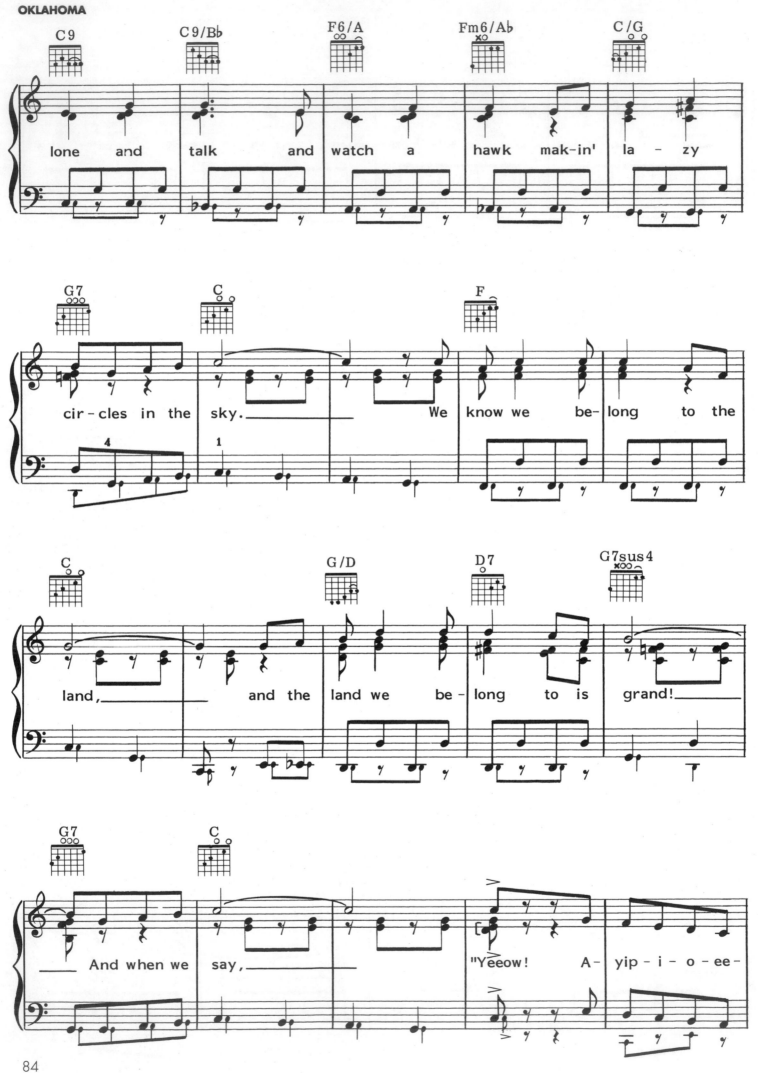

# OH, WHAT A BEAUTIFUL MORNIN'

There have been many songs extolling the beauties of the night — especially moonlit nights — but it took this opening song of *Oklahoma!* to undo the adverse musical reputation mornings had acquired several decades earlier with Irving Berlin's "Oh, How I Hate to Get Up in the Morning." Rodgers and Hammerstein's song not only got *Oklahoma!* off to a sunny start but went on to 15 consecutive weeks on *Your Hit Parade.* And Bing Crosby and Trudi Erwin's recording (backed by another *Oklahoma!* tune, "People Will Say We're in Love") went on to become one of the best-selling records of 1943.

**from *Oklahoma!*** Words by Oscar Hammerstein II; Music by Richard Rodgers

Bali Ha'i shares with Shangri-La the distinction of being one of the most exotic geographical locations in modern fiction. A creation of James Michener's imagination for his popular wartime book *Tales of the South Pacific* (two of its stories formed the basis of Rodgers and Hammerstein's 1949 Pulitzer Prize-winning *South Pacific*), Bali Ha'i is a mysterious Polynesian island where dreams supposedly come true. In the show the mystical island provides the idyllic setting for the meeting of a young American lieutenant and the beautiful Tonkinese girl with whom he falls in love. Perry Como and Jo Stafford both made hit recordings of the song soon after *South Pacific* opened on Broadway.

**from *South Pacific***     Words by Oscar Hammerstein II; Music by Richard Rodgers

88

Ha'i will whis-per on the wind of the sea: "Here am

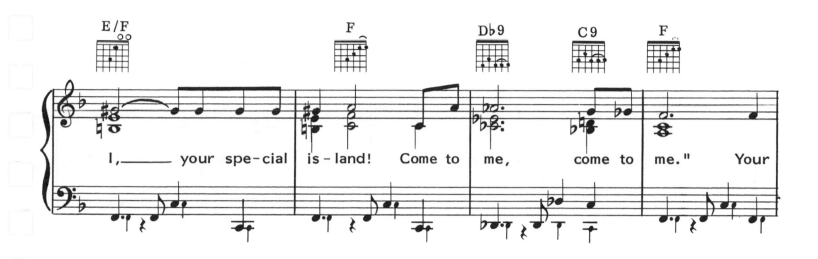

I,___ your spe-cial is-land! Come to me, come to me." Your

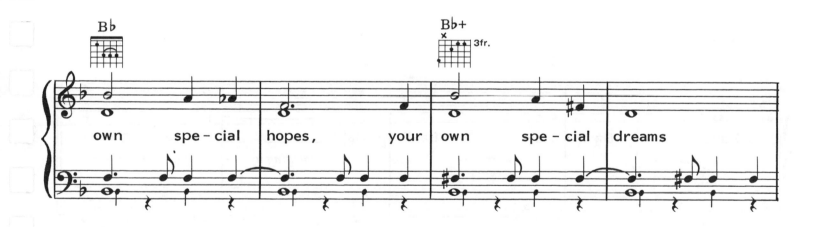

own spe-cial hopes, your own spe-cial dreams

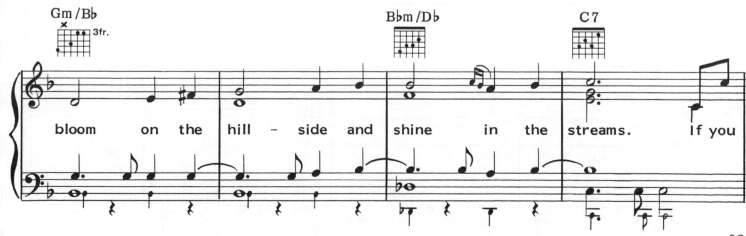

bloom on the hill-side and shine in the streams. If you

# A WONDERFUL GUY

Few songs so perfectly capture the joy and excitement of falling in love as Rodgers and Hammerstein's "A Wonderful Guy." It was introduced in *South Pacific* by Mary Martin in the role of Nellie Forbush, a young Navy nurse who falls in love with an older, aristocratic French planter (played by Metropolitan Opera bass-baritone Ezio Pinza). At first Nellie decides she's "Gonna Wash That Man Right Outa My Hair" (singing it in the shower, of course). But it's not long before she knows she's hooked and elatedly tells her fellow nurses how wonderful her guy is.

**from *South Pacific***   Words by Oscar Hammerstein II; Music by Richard Rodgers

# YOU'LL NEVER WALK ALONE

*Carousel*, in 1945, proved — for the first time since *Show Boat* in 1927 — that a serious, even tragic, story could provide the basis for a hit musical. Adapted from Hungarian writer Ferenc Molnar's play *Liliom*, *Carousel* tells of the romance of Billy Bigelow, a circus barker, and Julie Jordan, a New England mill-town girl. After Billy dies midway through the play, he returns to earth for one day to help his unhappy daughter. "You'll Never Walk Alone" is first sung in *Carousel* to comfort the hero's young widow, then reprised for the hopeful finale. Few musicals have provided as moving a tribute to faith in the brotherhood of man.

**from Carousel**     Words by Oscar Hammerstein II; Music by Richard Rodgers

Andante maestoso [with great warmth, like a hymn]

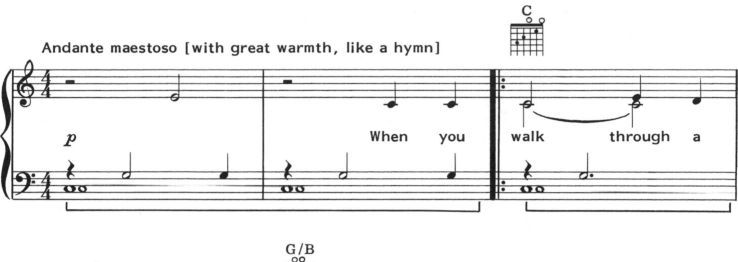

When you walk through a storm hold your head up high and

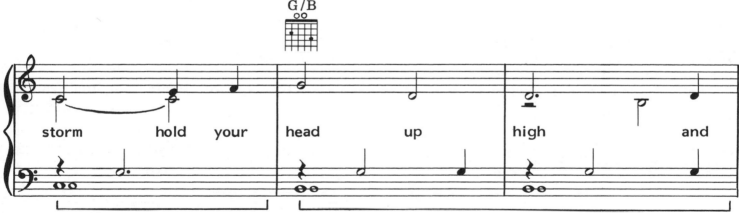

don't be a-fraid of the dark. At the

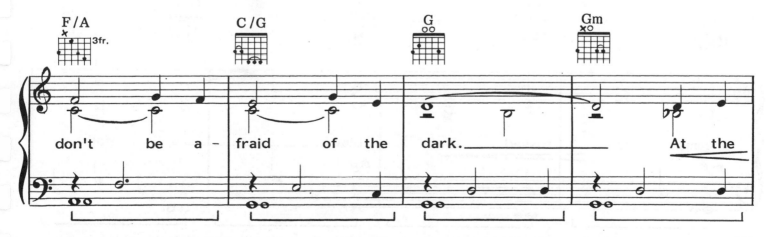

# THE COLE PORTER SHOWS

Most critics agree that Cole Porter never wrote a better score than that for *Kiss Me, Kate*. The show's most durable ballad remains the tender "So in Love," which stayed for 12 weeks on *Your Hit Parade* soon after the Broadway opening. The song establishes the true romantic feelings of the musical's battling hero and heroine — twice, in fact (midway in Act One and then for a full reprise in Act Two). Alfred Drake and Patricia Morison introduced it on Broadway in 1948, and Howard Keel and Kathryn Grayson sang it in the 1953 movie version (which, for reasons best known to MGM's brass, dropped the comma in the title).

Moderately, in 2 (♩ = 1 beat)     **from *Kiss Me, Kate***     Words and Music by Cole Porter

Strange, dear,— but true, dear,— when I'm close— to

you, dear,— the stars fill the sky,— so in

98

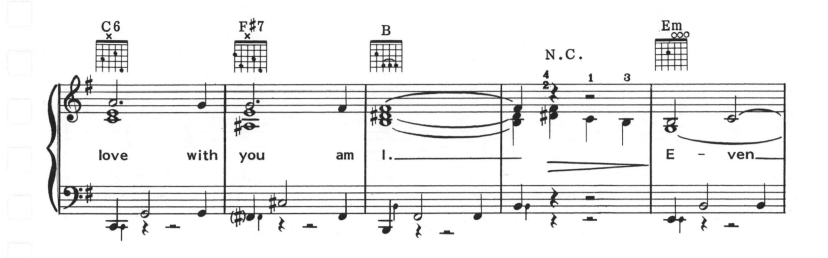

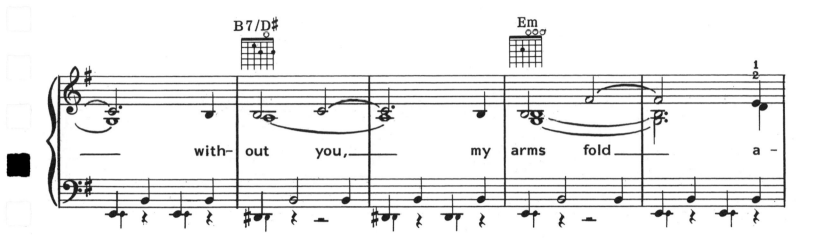

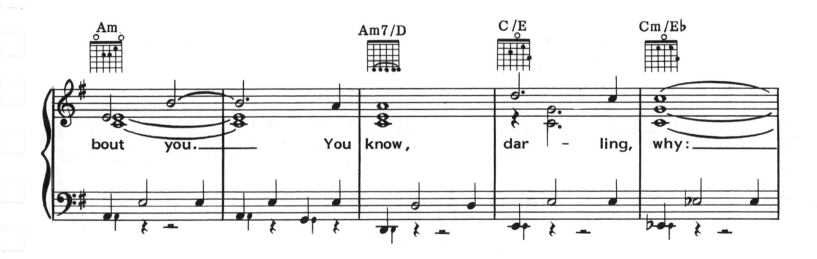

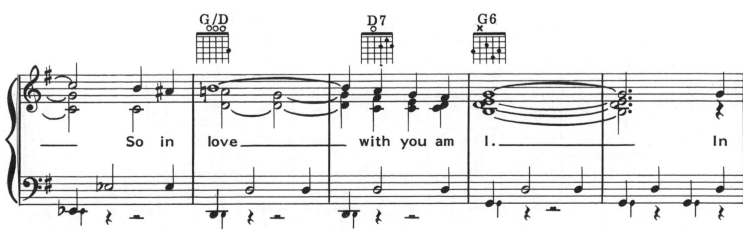

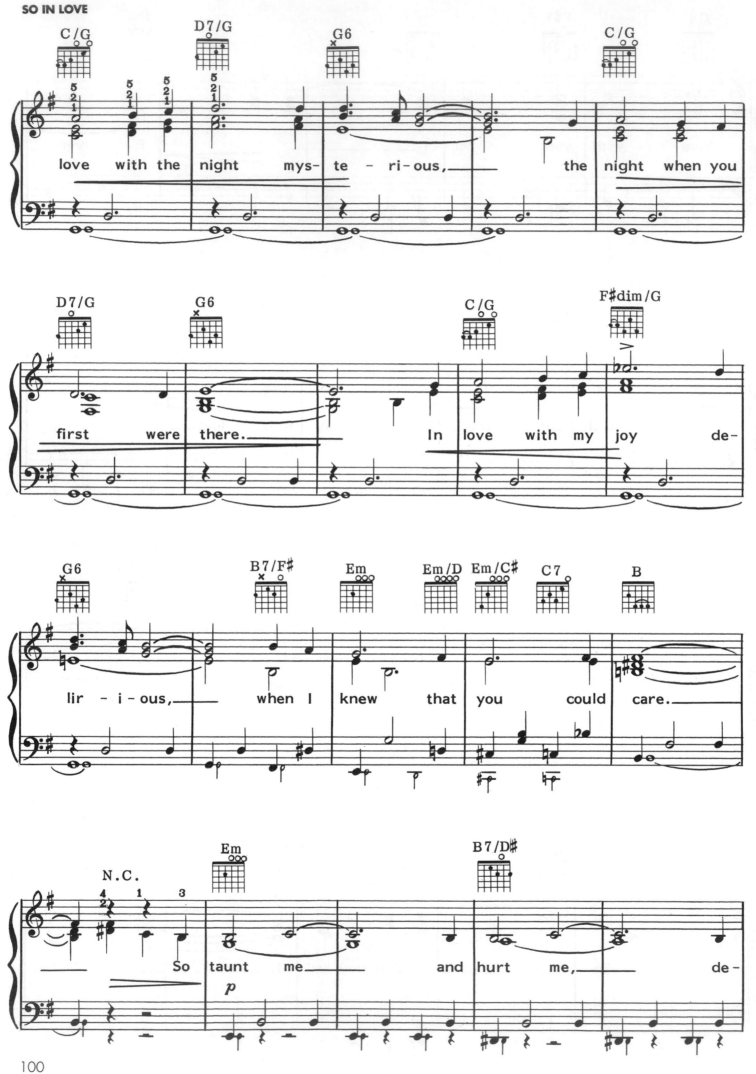

# C'EST MAGNIFIQUE

Cole Porter's love affair with Paris began in 1917 when he fled to France following the flop of his first Broadway musical, *See America First*. He maintained homes in both New York and the City of Light for several decades, and his first major Broadway success, in 1928, was titled — appropriately enough — *Paris*. But it was not until *Can-Can* in 1953 that Porter explicitly told the world "I Love Paris" in song. Both "I Love Paris" and the show's "C'Est Magnifique," sung by French star Lilo, went on to *Your Hit Parade*. In 1960 Frank Sinatra made "C'Est Magnifique" one of the highlights of the movie version of *Can-Can*.

**from Can-Can**     Words and Music by Cole Porter

But when, one day, your loved one drifts a-way, oo la la-la,—

it is so tra-gi-que.—
*(tra-zhee-kuh)*

But when; once

more, {he}{she} whis-pers, "Je t'a-dore," c'est mag-ni-fi
*(zhuh ta-door)*

**1.** que.

When

**2.** que.

*fading away*

*pp*

# IT'S ALL RIGHT WITH ME

*Can-Can* is a nostalgic bit of fiction about the introduction of can-can dancers in a turn-of-the-century music hall and how they divided and inflamed Paris's self-appointed moral guardians. Cole Porter himself fought many battles with American censors over the years, even to the point of having to substitute lyrics for some of his naughtier show tunes before they could be sung on radio, TV or in the movies. "It's All Right with Me," in which *Can-Can*'s hero admits "It's not *her* face, / but such a charming face / that it's all right with me," walks its moral tightrope so gracefully that it caused no problems. Peter Cookson sang the song on Broadway, Frank Sinatra in the film.

Very smoothly, in 2 (♩ = 1 beat)

**from Can-Can**  Words and Music by Cole Porter

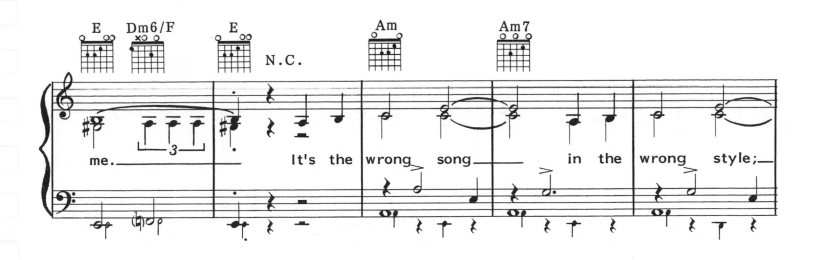

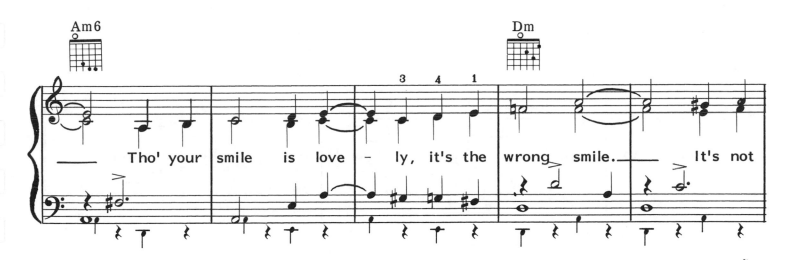

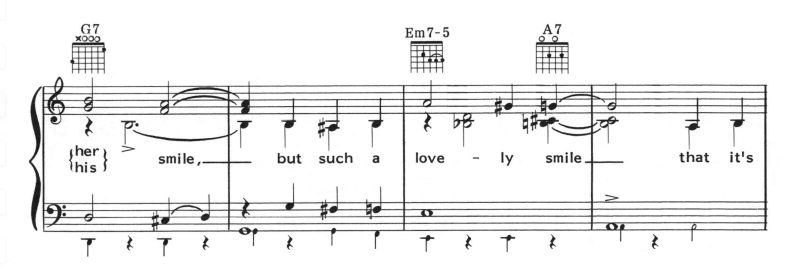

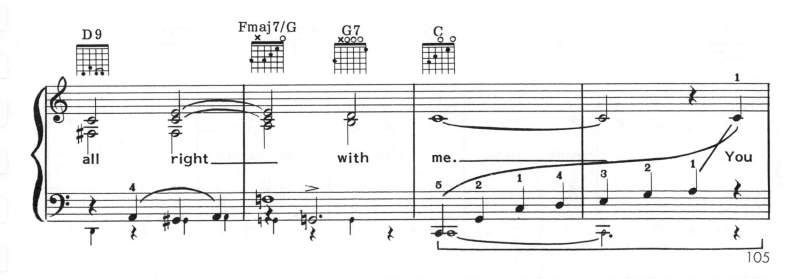

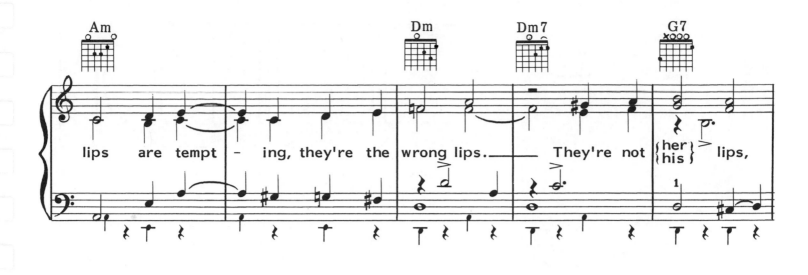

lips are tempt – ing, they're the wrong lips.__ They're not {her his} lips,

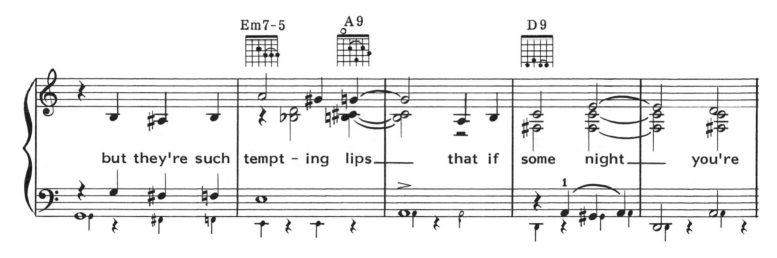

but they're such tempt – ing lips__ that if some night__ you're

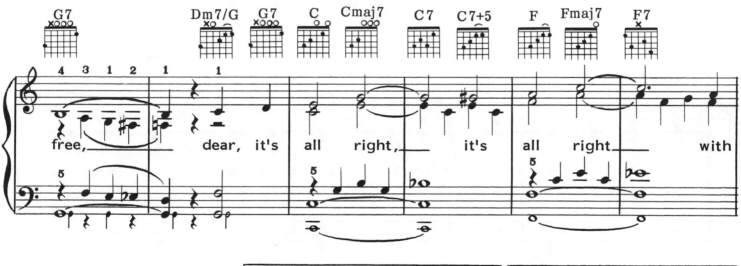

free,__ dear, it's all right,__ it's all right__ with

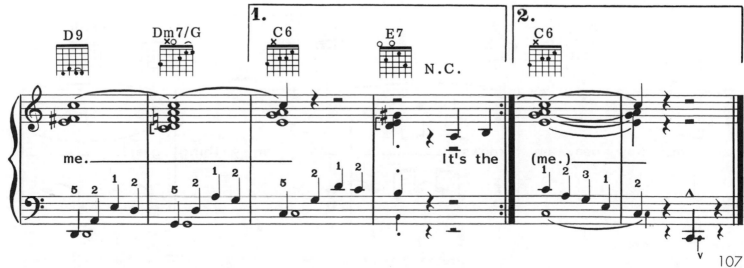

me.__ It's the (me.)__

# ANYTHING GOES

Originally a tongue-in-cheek takeoff on the moral climate of the early 1930s, the title song of *Anything Goes* has managed to speak, in one way or another, for just about every decade since then. Ethel Merman, in the role of nightclub singer Reno Sweeney, introduced it on Broadway in 1934 and also sang it in the film version two years later. The show itself has probably been revived successfully more times, including a smash-hit New York production in 1987, than any other Cole Porter musical.

**from *Anything Goes***    Words and Music by Cole Porter

Good au – thors, too, who once knew bet – ter words,

now on – ly use four-let – ter words writ-ing prose; _____ An-y-thing

goes! The world_ has gone mad to – day,_ and good's

bad to – day,_ and black's white to – day,_ and day's night to – day,_ when most

Cole Porter, whose witty, sophisticated songs have brought smiles to so many, spent most of his adult life disabled by a horseback-riding accident that left both of his legs shattered. The daily pain he endured was never reflected in his music—including that for his first Broadway hit after the accident, *Leave It to Me!*, in 1938. The production starred Victor Moore, William Gaxton and Sophie Tucker, but newcomer Mary Martin stole the show by dishing out a mock striptease in a fur coat as she coyly sang "My Heart Belongs to Daddy." She repeated her performance in the 1946 film biography of Porter, *Night and Day*.

# MY HEART BELONGS TO DADDY

**from Leave It to Me!**                    Words and Music by Cole Porter

# GET OUT OF TOWN

Question: When can a negative also be a positive? Answer: When a romantic Cole Porter lyric is involved — as in "Get Out of Town." Introduced by sultry singer Tamara (who had premiered Jerome Kern's "Smoke Gets In Your Eyes" in *Roberta* five years earlier), the song duplicitously urges a loved one to "Just disappear, / I care for you much too much." Although "My Heart Belongs to Daddy" stopped the show at every performance of *Leave It to Me!*, "Get Out of Town" became the musical's representative on *Your Hit Parade*. It has remained a popular standard ever since.

**from *Leave It to Me!***     Words and Music by Cole Porter

Get out of town

be - fore__ it's too late, my love;__

Get out of town,__ be good__ to me, please.__

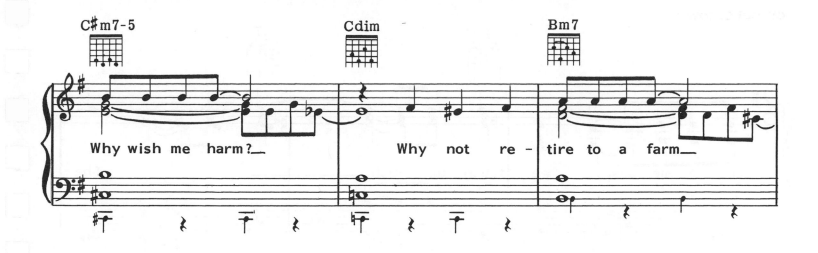

Why wish me harm?___ Why not re - tire to a farm___

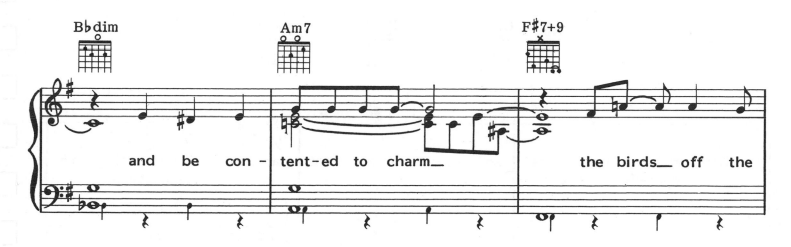

and be con - tent-ed to charm___ the birds___ off the

trees?___ Just dis-ap-pear,___ I care___ for you

much too much.___ And when you are near,___

# EV'RY TIME WE SAY GOODBYE

Producer Billy Rose's revue *Seven Lively Arts* (1944) combined songs by Cole Porter (sung by the likes of Dolores Gray and Nan Wynn), music by Igor Stravinsky (danced by ballet stars Alicia Markova and Anton Dolin), jazz numbers by "swing king" Benny Goodman and comedy sketches featuring Beatrice Lillie and Bert Lahr. Neither the critics nor audiences were enthusiastic about the mishmash. The show quickly closed. But "Ev'ry Time We Say Goodbye" became a hit. As Porter biographer Charles Schwartz wrote of the song: "Its simple, elegiac, repeated-note melody—a Porter characteristic—and cogent harmony beautifully complement a superior text."

**from *Seven Lively Arts***    Words and Music by Cole Porter

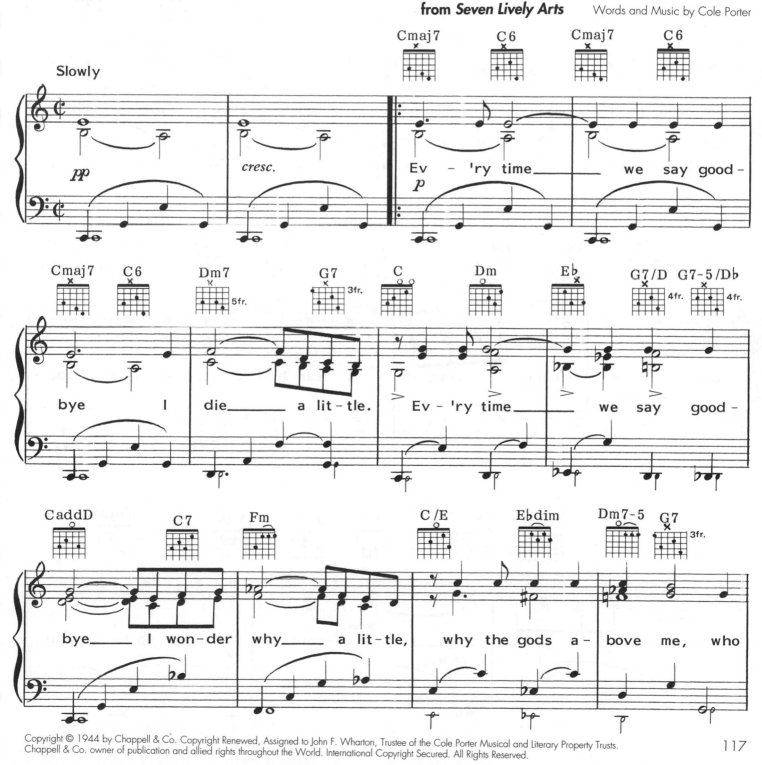

# NIGHT AND DAY

"Night and Day" has always been closely identified with Fred Astaire, who, when he first heard it, feared its range was too difficult for him. Finally, Cole Porter convinced Astaire he could handle the song—and it was "Night and Day" that turned 1932's *Gay Divorce* into Astaire's first solo hit without his longtime partner, sister Adele. The 1934 movie version not only changed the title to *The Gay Divorcee* (in the interests of propriety: divorcees might be gay, but not divorces), but it also scrapped all of the original show's songs except "Night and Day." This haunting melody, of course, became the basis for one of the most famous of movie dance sequences done by Fred and his new partner, Ginger Rogers.

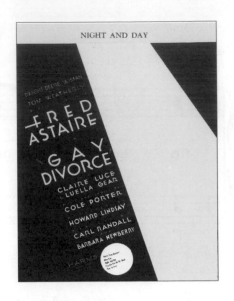

**Moderately**

**from *Gay Divorce***          Words and Music by Cole Porter

Like the beat, beat, beat of the tom-tom when the jun-gle shad-ows fall, like the tick, tick, tock of the state-ly clock as it stands a-gainst the wall, like the drip, drip, drip of the rain-drops when the sum-mer show'r is through, so a voice with-in me keeps re-peat-ing, you, you, you!

# YOU'RE THE TOP

Few popular songs have had as many lyrics amended or appended over the years as this most clever of "list songs"—some by Cole Porter himself, some by other lyricists (with and without Porter's consent). The original version of "You're the Top," used here, was a showstopper for Ethel Merman and William Gaxton in *Anything Goes* in 1934 — with its topical references to Greta Garbo, Mickey Mouse, Jimmy Durante, cellophane, hats from Henri Bendel's in New York and much more. The 1936 film version (with Merman and Bing Crosby) inserted references to Gershwin, Einstein, Dizzy Dean and Ford V-8s— and numerous other "updates" have appeared through the years.

**from *Anything Goes***   Words and Music by Cole Porter

*Light and swingy*

He: At words po-et-ic I'm so pa-thet-ic that I al-ways have found it
She: (Your) words po-et-ic are not pa-thet-ic. On the oth-er hand, boy, you

best, in-stead of get-ting 'em off my chest, to let 'em
shine. And I can feel af-ter ev-'ry line a thrill di-

rest un-ex-pressed. I hate pa-rad-ing my ser-e-nad-ing as I'll
vine down my spine. Now gift-ed hu-mans like Vin-cent You-mans might

*Chorus 3*

You're the top!
You're an Arrow collar.
You're the top!
You're a Coolidge dollar.
You're the nimble tread of the feet of Fred Astaire.
You're an O'Neill drama,
You're Whistler's mama,
You're Camembert.
You're a rose,
You're Inferno's Dante,
You're the nose
On the great Durante.
I'm just in the way, as the French would say,
   "De trop."
But if, baby, I'm the bottom,
You're the top.

*Chorus 4*

You're the top!
You're a Waldorf salad.
You're the top!
You're a Berlin ballad.
You're a baby grand of a lady
   and a gent.
You're an old Dutch master,
You're Mrs. Astor,
You're Pepsodent.
You're romance.
You're the steppes of Russia.
You're the pants on a Roxy usher.
I'm a lazy lout that's just about
   to stop.
But if, baby, I'm the bottom,
You're the top.

*Chorus 5*

You're the top!
You're a dance in Bali.
You're the top!
You're a hot tamale.
You're an angel, you, simply too, too,
   too diveen.
You're a Botticelli,
You're Keats,
You're Shelley,
You're Ovaltine.
You're a boon,
You're the dam at Boulder.
You're the moon over Mae West's shoulder.
I'm a nominee of the G.O.P. or GOP.
But if, baby, I'm the bottom,
You're the top.

# ALL OF YOU

Broadway show conductor Maurice Levine argues that Cole Porter, besides, of course, being witty and sophisticated, was also the most openly passionate of the Golden Age songwriters. Levine cites the lyrics of "Night and Day," "I've Got You Under My Skin" and "All of You" to bolster his point. The lustily ardent "All of You" is from Porter's *Silk Stockings*. Don Ameche sang the song to Hildegard Knef (a.k.a. Hildegarde Neff) in the original 1955 Broadway production, and Fred Astaire to Cyd Charisse in the 1957 film version.

**from *Silk Stockings***      Words and Music by Cole Porter

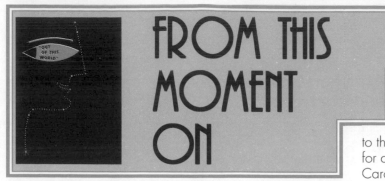

# FROM THIS MOMENT ON

When the notices for Cole Porter's *Out of This World* indicated trouble during the show's pre-Broadway run in 1950, several songs, including "From This Moment On," were cut before the musical reached New York — and mixed reviews. Nonetheless, "From This Moment On," because of its catchy melody and ebullient lyrics, became a favorite of supper club and radio singers. In 1953 it was added to the movie version of Porter's *Kiss Me, Kate* and set the scene for a breathtaking dance sequence by Ann Miller, Bob Fosse, Carol Haney, Bobby Van, Jeanne Coyne and Tommy Rall.

**from *Out of This World***　　　Words and Music by Cole Porter

Bright and spirited, in 2 (♩ = 1 beat)

From this mo - ment on,_____ you for
From this hap - py day,_____ no more

me, dear, on - ly two for tea, dear,
blue songs, on - ly whoop-dee - doo songs,

1. from this mo - ment on._____

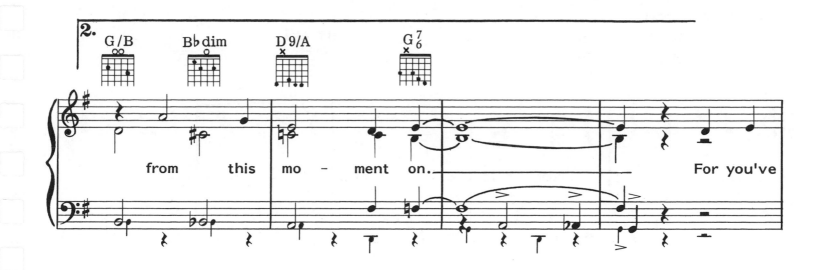

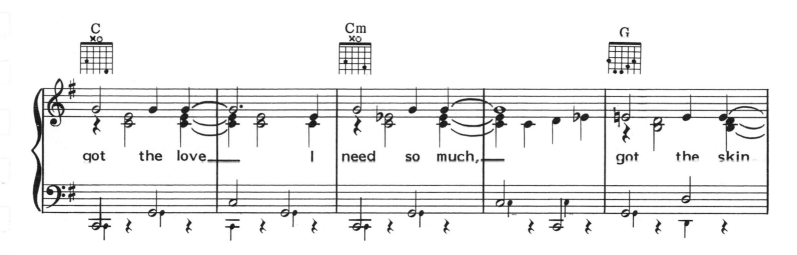

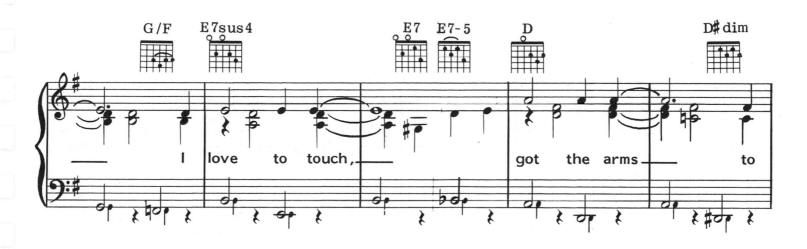

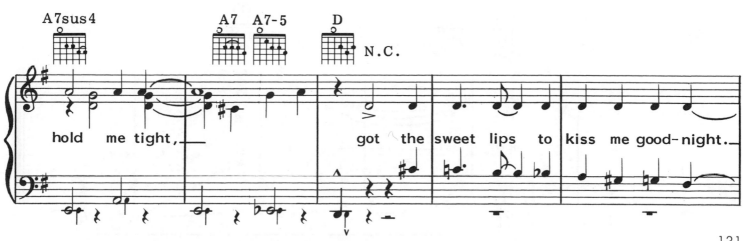

# EARLY, EVERLASTING SHOW TUNES FROM 1905 TO 1929

# YOU'RE THE CREAM IN MY COFFEE

Just as "Tea for Two" really has little to do with tea, so "You're the Cream in My Coffee" has little to do with coffee. Instead, coffee merely heads a list of everyday things that are taken for granted (or *were* in 1928, anyway) and that the singer equates with the qualities of his or her loved one. Jack Whiting and Ona Munson introduced the song as a duet in the revue *Hold Everything!,* which also starred Bert Lahr and Victor Moore. The tune was also woven into the 1929 movie comedy *Cock-Eyed World,* in which Victor McLaglen and Edmund Lowe reprised their *What Price Glory?* roles as the battling sergeants Flagg and Quirt.

**from *Hold Everything!***     Words and Music by B.G. DeSylva, Lew Brown and Ray Henderson

# Tea for Two

"Tea for Two" was a last-minute addition to *No, No, Nanette* during the show's pre-Broadway run in Chicago (in April of 1924). Irving Caesar tossed off the lyrics in less than ten minutes, fully intending to rework them before the New York opening. Somehow the "temporary" lyrics never were changed. But Vincent Youmans' instantly hummable tune and the basic romantic thrust of the opening lyric of the song's refrain ("Picture you upon my knee…") were enough to turn "Tea for Two" into a big hit. They were also enough to make the song a centerpiece of the many revivals of *No, No, Nanette* over the years.

**from *No, No, Nanette***      Words by Irving Caesar; Music by Vincent Youmans

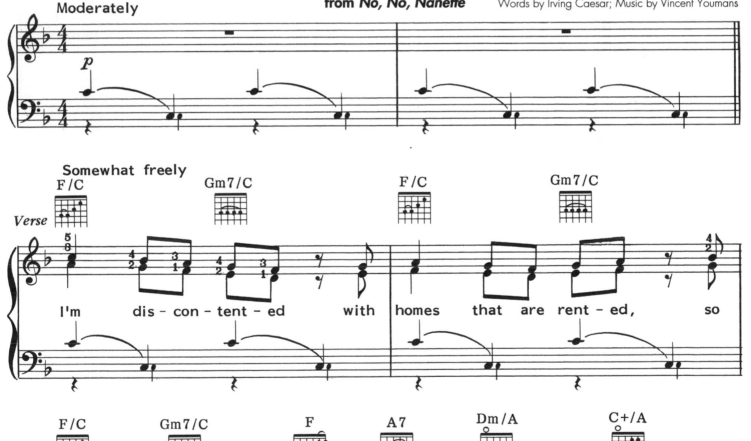

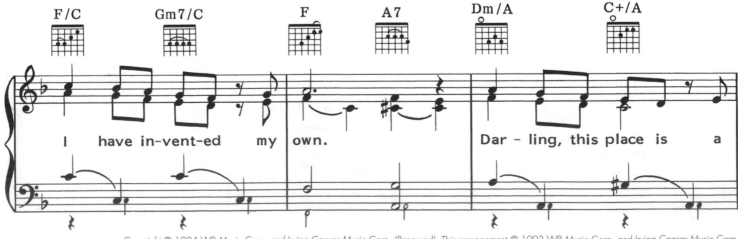

I'm dis-con-tent-ed with homes that are rent-ed, so

I have in-vent-ed my own. Dar-ling, this place is a

**TEA FOR TWO**

139

# MAKIN' WHOOPEE

Singer-comedian Eddie Cantor introduced this double-entendred song in 1928 — and turned it into one of the biggest hits of his lengthy career on the stage, in movies, on radio and on television. Ironically, producer Florenz Ziegfeld had something closer to the term "whoop it up" in mind, especially as applied to Native American celebrations, when he put Cantor and Ziegfeld's chorines in Arizona cowboy-and-Indian territory in *Whoopee*. But Gus Kahn's lyrics and Cantor's wry, show-stopping delivery of them transformed the meaning of the expression literally overnight.

**from Whoopee**

Words by Gus Kahn; Music by Walter Donaldson

With sly good humor

# MY BABY JUST CARES FOR ME

The 1930 screen adaptation of Florenz Ziegfeld's *Whoopee* is historic in several ways. First, it made a movie star of Eddie Cantor. Second, it was the first major film to be choreographed by the now-legendary Busby Berkeley. And, third, it was one of the first musicals to be filmed entirely in an early Technicolor process. Although the movie retained most of the original Broadway cast, producer Samuel Goldwyn did away with much of the original Walter Donaldson–Gus Kahn score. One of the new songs he commissioned, "My Baby Just Cares for Me," became so popular after the movie's release that it was added to later stage revivals of *Whoopee*, including the Goodspeed Opera production that moved to Broadway in 1979.

**from Whoopee**     Words by Gus Kahn; Music by Walter Donaldson

143

* *John Gilbert (1895-1936), silent-film star.*
** *Lawrence Tibbett (1896-1960), American operatic baritone.*

# GIVE MY REGARDS TO BROADWAY

For the first several decades of this century, George M. Cohan was to Broadway musicals what Charlie Chaplin was to movie comedy: the undisputed master. Not only was he star, writer, composer, director and producer of most of his shows, he was also one of the first to stress the "American-ness" of his productions (in contrast to the European operetta models of Victor Herbert and others). Even when Cohan set a show abroad, as with 1904's *Little Johnny Jones* (about an American jockey in England), he featured bravura pieces of pure Americana: "Give My Regards to Broadway" and "The Yankee Doodle Boy." "Give My Regards to Broadway" will forever be a magnificent tribute to the Great White Way.

**from *Little Johnny Jones***    Words and Music by George M. Cohan

# I Love a Piano

When Irving Berlin wrote this song in 1915, the piano was *the* popular family instrument. Having a piano in the parlor was as much a status symbol as having a TV set or VCR years later. Even families that couldn't afford to buy a piano could always rent one (for about a dollar a month), and neighborhood piano lessons were abundantly available (often for only 25 cents an hour). So there were plenty of folks who quickly adopted Berlin's "I Love a Piano" as their own when it was introduced in Charles Dillingham's revue *Stop! Look! Listen!* Years later, Judy Garland sang the song in one of her most popular movies, *Easter Parade.*

**from Stop! Look! Listen!**　　　　　　Words and Music by Irving Berlin

* *A green Tetrazine = an unskilled singer (after Luisa Tetrazzini [1871-1940], the great operatic soprano).*

149

*Ignace Paderewski (1860-1941), Polish piano virtuoso and statesman.*

way.___ I'm so de-light-ed___ if I'm in-vit-ed___ to hear that

long-haired gen-ius play.___ So you can keep your fid-dle

and your bow; Give me a P - I - A - N - O. Oh, oh, I love to

stop right___ be-side an up-right or a high-toned ba-by

**1.** grand. When a

**2.** grand.

# KISS ME AGAIN
# KISS ME AGAIN
# KISS ME AGAIN
# KISS ME AGAIN

When Rodgers and Hammerstein's "Some Enchanted Evening" turned Metropolitan Opera basso Ezio Pinza into a Broadway star, it was repeating, in a way, what "Kiss Me Again" had done for Met soprano Fritzi Scheff nearly five decades earlier. Scheff was such a hit singing the sensuous waltz in her 1905 Broadway debut that she became intensely identified with it, more so than with any of her operatic roles. Victor Herbert later wrote two other operettas for Scheff (*The Prima Donna* and *The Duchess*), but neither quite matched the success of *Mlle. Modiste*. A movie version was made in 1931 with Bernice Claire and Walter Pidgeon — and, significantly, the film's title was changed to *Kiss Me Again,* to reflect the show's most durable song hit.

**from *Mlle. Modiste***     Words by Henry Blossom; Music by Victor Herbert

Sweet sum-mer breeze, whis-per-ing trees, stars shin-ing soft - ly a-bove. Ros-es in bloom, waft-ed per-fume,

It's not unusual for one hit song to survive a flop show, but *Great Day!* had three that ended up on *Variety*'s Top Ten list in early 1930: the rousing title song, the romantic ballad "More Than You Know" and this compelling tribute to the power of music. Composer Vincent Youmans considered "Without a Song" so immortal that he insisted showman-lyricist Billy Rose be more formally identified as "William" in the song's credits. And Metropolitan Opera baritone Lawrence Tibbett liked "Without a Song" so much that he sang it in his 1931 movie *The Prodigal*. The song's assertion that "when things go wrong, a man ain't got a friend without a song" struck a particularly responsive chord in those early Depression days — and continues to express the value of music in helping people through all sorts of personal difficulties.

**from *Great Day!***          Words by Edward Eliscu and William Rose; Music by Vincent Youmans

155

**WITHOUT A SONG**

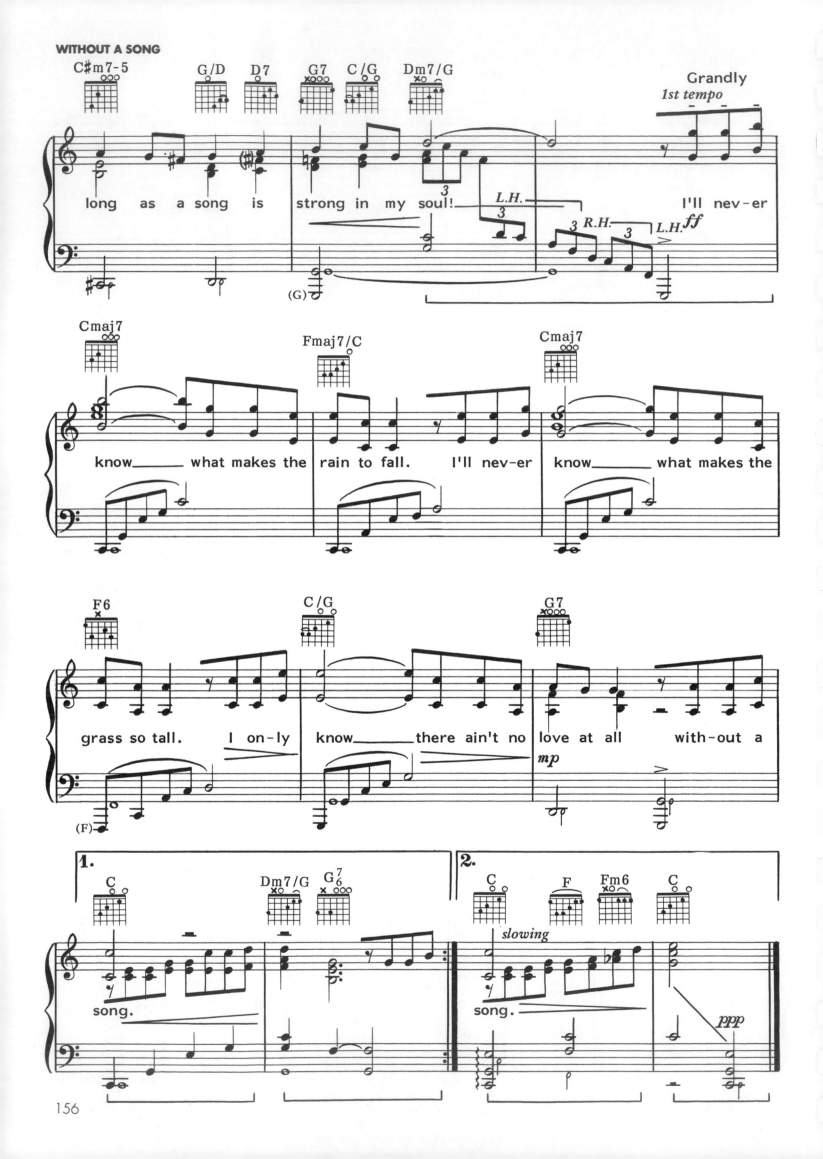

# THE SOARING MELODIES OF JEROME KERN

Helen Morgan introduced "Bill" in the original 1927 production of *Show Boat*. But the song's history goes back a decade before that, to the musical *Oh, Lady! Lady!!* "Bill" was not only dropped from that show before the New York opening, but also from *Zip Goes a Million* in 1919 and *Sally* in 1920. When a song was needed for Morgan's character in *Show Boat*, Jerome Kern suggested this one. Oscar Hammerstein II altered some 16 bars of the original lyrics by P.G. Wodehouse (yes, *that* P.G. Wodehouse) and incorporated "Bill" into the show. Despite the fact that Hammerstein is listed as co-lyricist, he always insisted that the song be credited fully to Wodehouse.

**from *Show Boat***  Words by P.G. Wodehouse and Oscar Hammerstein II; Music by Jerome Kern

**Moderately and freely throughout**

I used to dream that I would dis- cov- er_____ the per- fect
He can't play golf or ten- nis or po- lo_____ or sing a

lov- er some day. I knew I'd rec-og- nize him if
so- lo or row. He is- n't half as hand- some as

ev- er he came 'round my way. I
doz- ens of men that I know. He al- ways used to
is- n't tall and

# Nobody Else But Me

In planning the 1946 Broadway revival of *Show Boat*, Jerome Kern and Oscar Hammerstein decided a new song was needed for the last act. The new tune, "Nobody Else But Me," sung in the revival by Jan Clayton as Magnolia Hawks Ravenal (Norma Terris was the original Magnolia), turned out to be the last one Kern ever wrote. The composer died of a cerebral hemorrhage two months before the revival opened. "Nobody Else But Me" was dropped from the national tour of *Show Boat* in 1948, because of road expenses, and was also dropped from MGM's 1951 movie remake. But it did make it into a 1971 London revival, although transferred to another character and moved up to Act I.

**from *Show Boat***  Words by Oscar Hammerstein II; Music by Jerome Kern

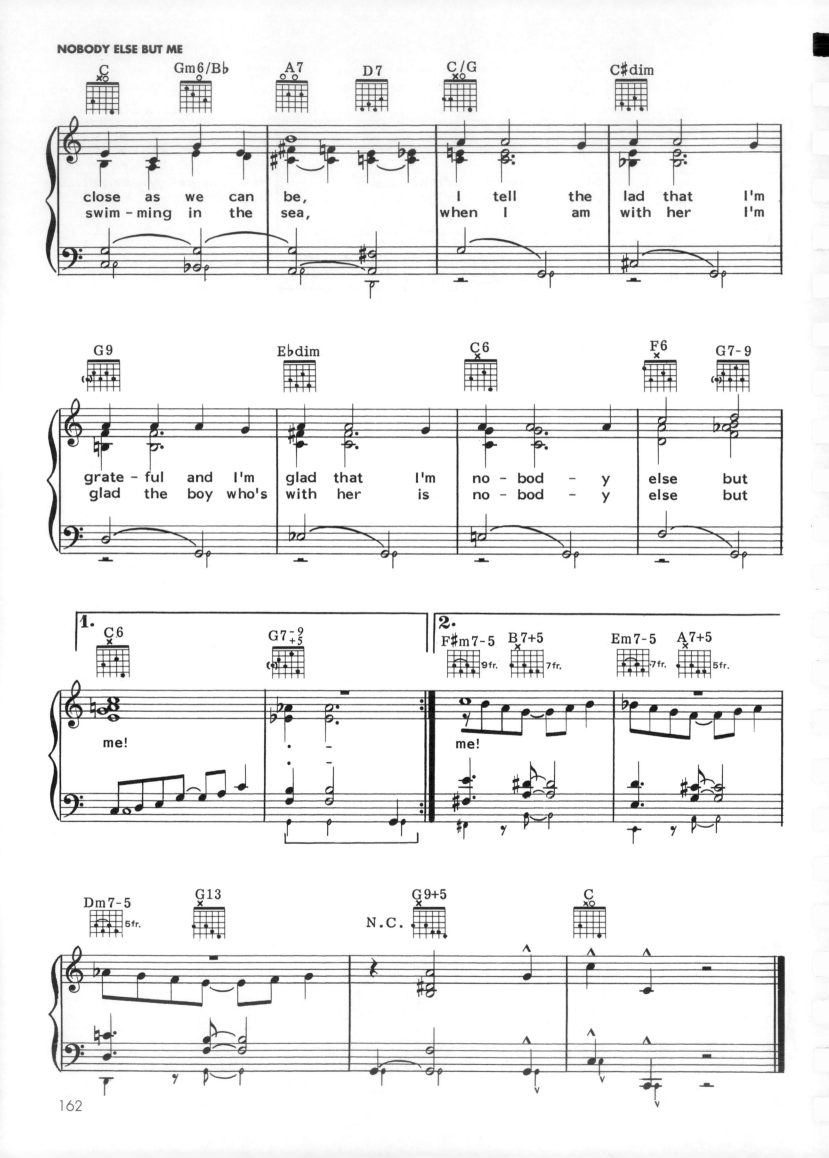

In an echo of *Romeo and Juliet's* balcony scene, the romance in *Show Boat* between riverboat gambler Gaylord Ravenal and Magnolia, the daughter of the show boat's captain, begins when Ravenal (standing on the levee) spots Magnolia on the boat's upper deck and asks if she's an actress. No, she replies, but she would love to be one because an actress "can make believe so many wonderful things that never happen in real life." Ravenal suggests they make believe in song that they've fallen in love at first sight — and they do just that to one of Jerome Kern's most melting melodies. Irene Dunne and Allan Jones sang "Make Believe" in the 1936 film version of *Show Boat,* and Kathryn Grayson and Howard Keel in the 1951 remake.

**from Show Boat**

Words by Oscar Hammerstein II; Music by Jerome Kern

164    *Kern insisted that this word be used instead of "Chorus."*

# ALL THE THINGS YOU ARE

Many musicians consider "All the Things You Are" Jerome Kern's crowning achievement. Composer Arthur Schwartz went so far as to call the tune from *Very Warm for May* (1939) "the greatest song ever written." Ironically, Kern originally thought the song—with its subtle key changes and, after a simple beginning, a relatively complex development—might be too sophisticated for popular audiences. But thanks in part to recordings by the Tommy Dorsey, Artie Shaw and Freddy Martin orchestras, "All the Things You Are" caught on quickly. When the song stayed for weeks on *Your Hit Parade* (including two in the No.1 spot), no one was more surprised than the composer. "All the Things You Are" has remained a memorable favorite ever since.

**from *Very Warm for May*** Words by Oscar Hammerstein II; Music by Jerome Kern

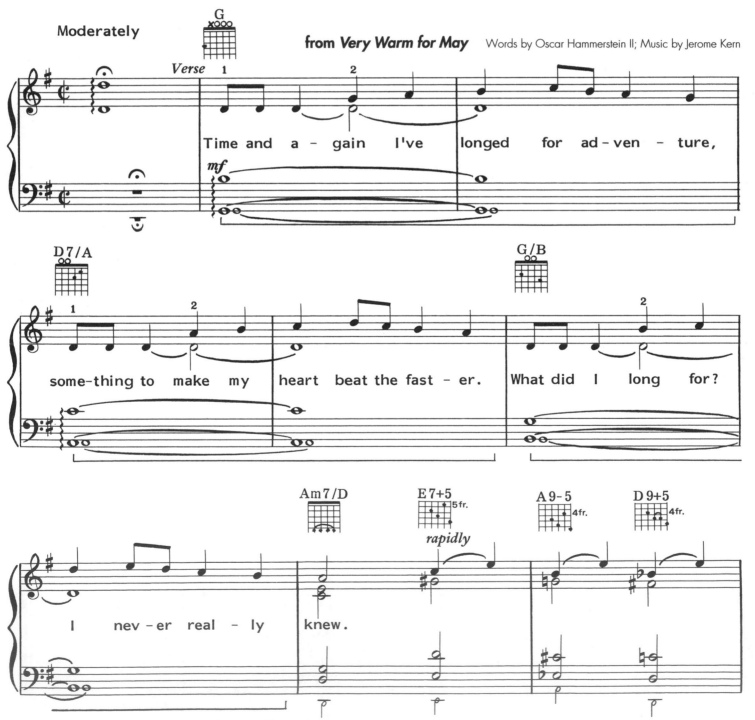

Time and a-gain I've longed for ad-ven-ture, some-thing to make my heart beat the fast-er. What did I long for? I nev-er real-ly knew.

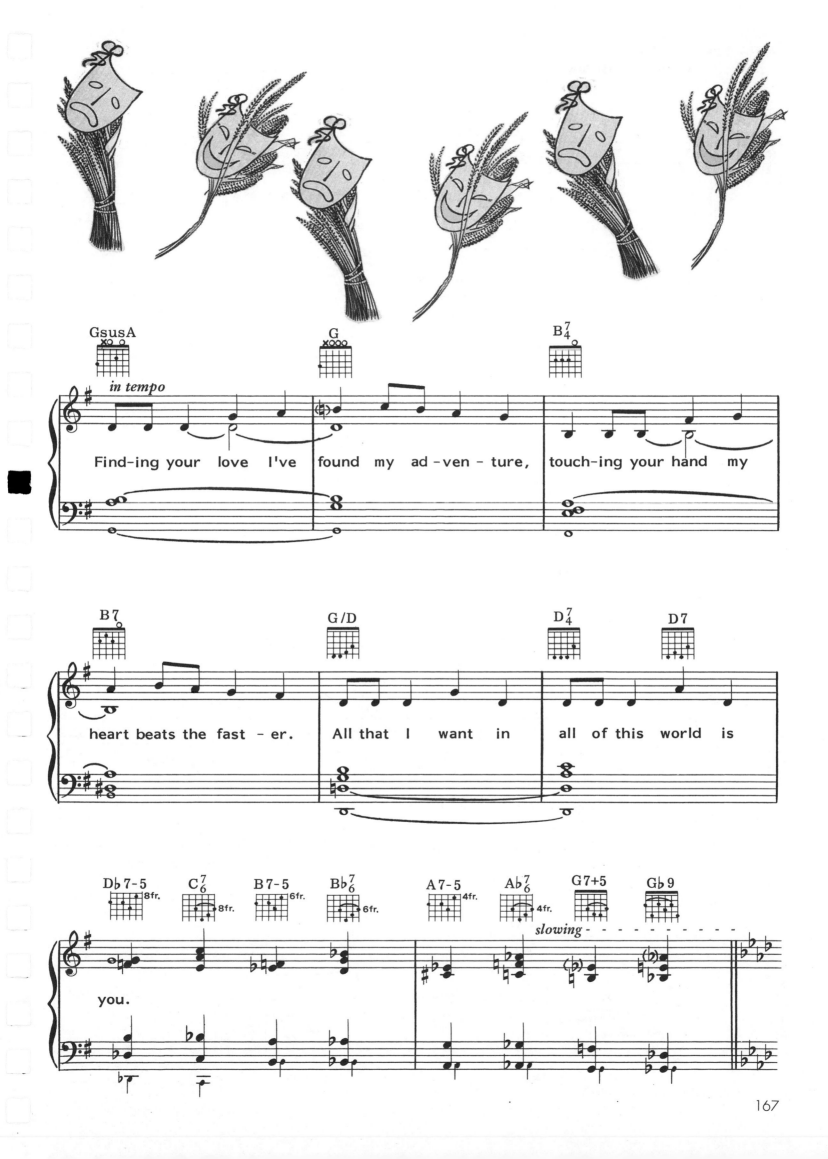

**ALL THE THINGS YOU ARE**

*Jerome Kern's name for "Chorus."*

# LOOK FOR THE SILVER LINING

"Look for the Silver Lining" was written for 1919's *Zip Goes a Million*, which flopped. The following year it was put into *Sally*, a Cinderella-style tale about a dishwasher who becomes a star in the *Ziegfeld Follies*. The Ziegfeld-produced *Sally* made a star of Marilyn Miller, who re-created the role for the 1930 movie version. When June Haver played Miller in a considerably whitewashed 1949 film biography, "Look for the Silver Lining" provided not only the film's title but also its final production number. The song was featured in the 1946 Kern bio-pic, *Till the Clouds Roll By*, in which Judy Garland (as Marilyn Miller) sings an unforgettably wistful version.

**from *Sally***    Words by Buddy DeSylva; Music by Jerome Kern

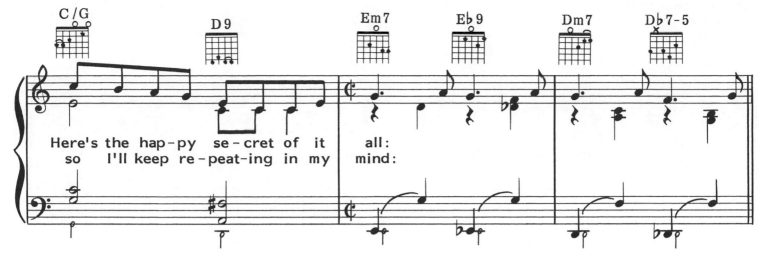

Here's the hap-py se-cret of it all:
so I'll keep re-peat-ing in my mind:

all:
mind:

**Very smooth and steady**

*Chorus*

*mp-mf*

Look for ____ the sil - ver lin - ing ____

when - e'er a cloud ap - pears in the

blue. ____ Re - mem - ber, some - where ____

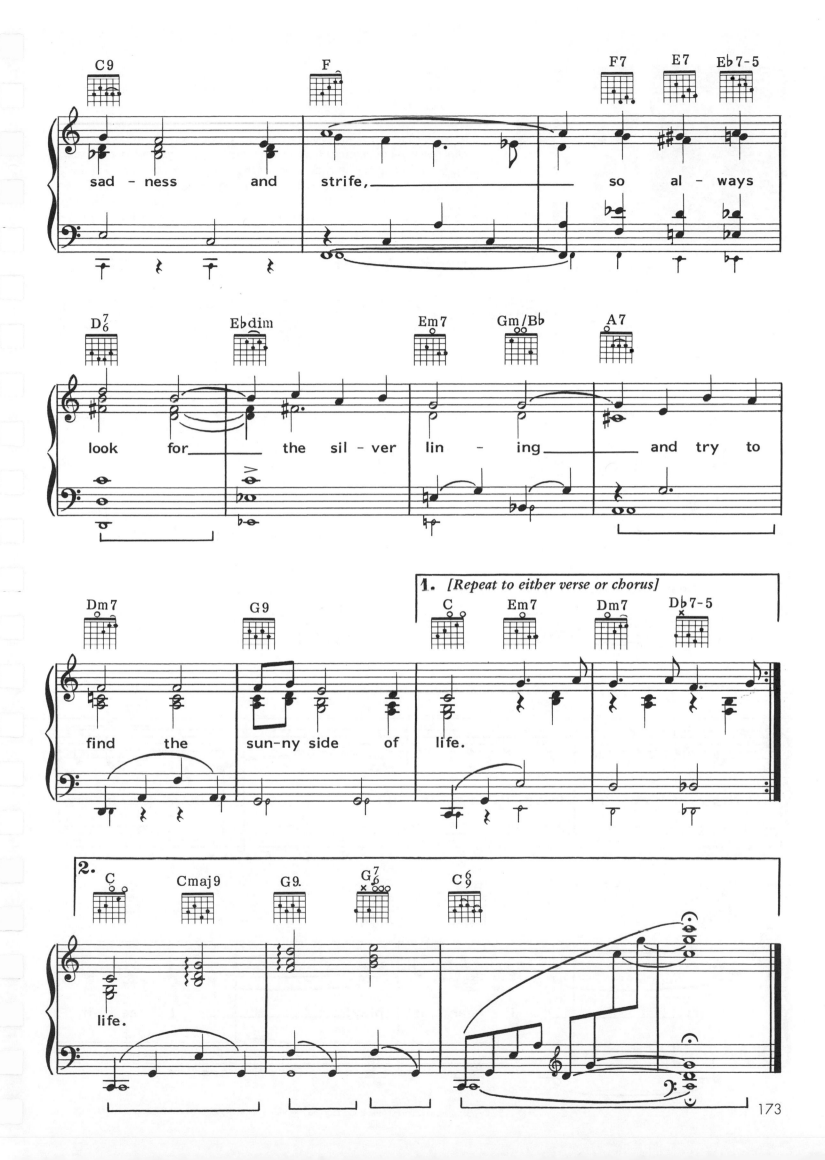

173

# THE SONG IS YOU

The 1932 Broadway hit *Music in the Air* was Jerome Kern's sophisticated switch on old-fashioned Middle European-set operettas—with the pretty country lass *not* succeeding this time when she's hired by a theater impresario to replace the temperamental prima donna. Also unique at the time was the show's rhymed and metered dialogue, and Kern's almost continuous musical underscoring, culminating in the rhapsodic duet "The Song Is You" (sung by the show's two stars, Tullio Carminati and Natalie Hall). When *Music in the Air* was made into a movie in 1934 (with Gloria Swanson and John Boles), "The Song Is You" was inexplicably cut, in keeping with Hollywood's seemingly perverse treatment of Broadway adaptations at that time.

**from *Music in the Air***    Words by Oscar Hammerstein II; Music by Jerome Kern

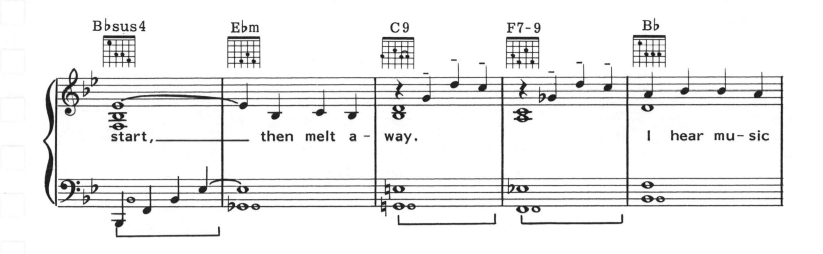

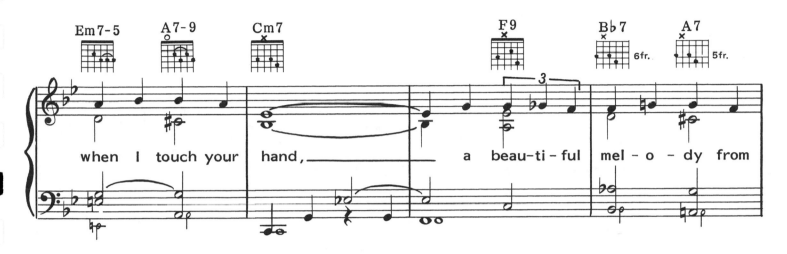

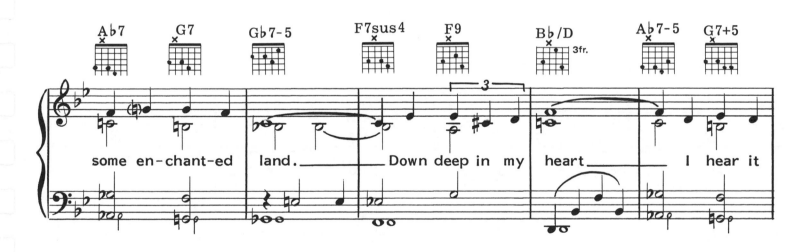

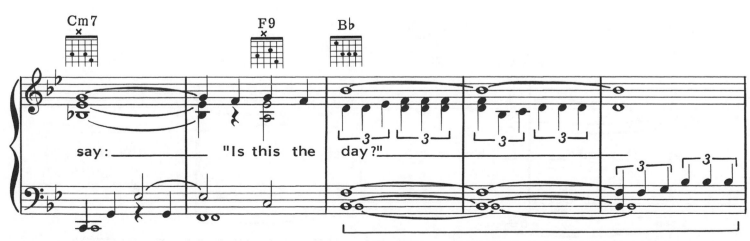

# SMOKE GETS IN YOUR EYES

The plaintive "Smoke Gets In Your Eyes" is one of the most famous of all songs about a lost love— a love that's gone up, metaphorically speaking, in a puff of smoke. What most people don't know is that Jerome Kern originally wrote the melody in march time as a theme for a proposed radio show. When the program was never produced, Kern slowed down the tempo and reworked the song. Singer-actress Tamara introduced it in *Roberta* in 1933. Irene Dunne sang it in the 1935 film version, followed by as elegant an adagio as Fred Astaire and Ginger Rogers ever danced. In 1958 The Platters spearheaded a hit revival that landed "Smoke Gets In Your Eyes" on *Your Hit Parade* for 12 weeks.

**from *Roberta***　　Words by Otto Harbach; Music by Jerome Kern

*They asked me how I knew my true love was true.____ I, of course, replied, "Something here inside cannot be denied." They said, "Someday you'll*

*\* Small notes are for singers with more limited ranges only. Do not play them on piano.*

# GEORGE GERSHWIN AND HAROLD ARLEN: BLUE NOTES ON BROADWAY

## LIZA
### (All the Clouds'll Roll Away)

Dixie Dugan, the fictional Broadway hopeful of *Liberty* magazine stories (and later a comic-strip character), was the heroine of 1929's *Show Girl*. For the role, Florenz Ziegfeld chose 19-year-old dancer Ruby Keeler, who had recently married 42-year-old Al Jolson. Ziegfeld asked the Gershwins to write a minstrel-style number for Keeler and singer Nick Lucas. They obliged with "Liza." On opening night, Jolson, sitting in a third-row aisle seat, suddenly jumped up during that number and began singing the song to his bride. The audience went wild. Jolson, with Ziegfeld's blessing, repeated his "spontaneous serenade" on other nights. When he returned to Hollywood, *Show Girl* closed. But "Liza" remained a lasting part of Jolson's repertoire.

**Moderate swing**       **from *Show Girl***       Words by Ira Gershwin and Gus Kahn; Music by George Gershwin

# SOMEONE TO WATCH OVER ME

Long popular as one of the most romantic of all Gershwin songs, "Someone to Watch Over Me" began its compositional life as an up-tempo tune. But then George and Ira decided to slow it down and turn it into a ballad for the 1926 musical comedy *Oh, Kay!* Gertrude Lawrence introduced it in that show, singing it alone onstage to a rag doll—similar to a number she had done in London in *Charlot's Revue of 1924* (singing there with a Pierrot doll to Noel Coward's "Parisian Pierrot"). "Someone to Watch Over Me" quickly became one of *Oh, Kay!*'s hits, along with "Do, Do, Do" and "Clap Yo' Hands."

*Verse:* **Ad lib.** (relaxed phrasing ♪♪ = ♪³♪)

**from *Oh, Kay!***

Words by Ira Gershwin; Music by George Gershwin

There's a say-ing old says that love is blind. Still, we're of-ten told, "Seek and ye shall find." So I'm going to seek a cer-tain lad I've had in mind. Look-ing ev-'ry-where, have-n't found him yet.

He's the big af-fair I can-not for-get. On - ly man I

ev-er think of with re-gret. I'd like to

add his in-i-tial to my mon-o-gram.__ Tell me,

where is the shep-herd for this lost lamb?

185

*Chorus:* In tempo, slow ballad

There's a some-bod-y I'm long-ing to see. I hope that he turns out to be some-one who'll watch o - ver me.

I'm a lit-tle lamb who's lost in the wood. I know I could al-ways be good to one who'll watch o - ver me. Al-though he may not be the

Delicately, like a music box*

*Both bands may be played an 8va higher till *

# HE LOVES AND SHE LOVES

The history of music is filled with songs based on bits and pieces of earlier ones. "He Loves and She Loves" is such a work. In 1919 George Gershwin wrote "Something About Love" with lyricist Lou Paley for the short-lived *The Lady in Red*. Ira Gershwin liked the way Paley ended the song with "I love and you love, he loves and she loves." When George and Ira needed a song for *Funny Face* in 1927, they reworked (with Paley's consent) the last eight bars of "Something About Love" with a melody from a discarded earlier version of "The Man I Love." And so the lovely "He Loves and She Loves" was born. It's probably best remembered today for the sequence in which Fred Astaire sings it to Audrey Hepburn in the 1957 film *Funny Face*. (Although Fred had also starred in the show, 30 years earlier, his sister, Adele, and Allen Kearns sang the song then.)

**from *Funny Face***     Words by Ira Gershwin; Music by George Gershwin

Although recognized today as one of the Gershwins' all-time most popular songs, "The Man I Love" spent the first few years of its existence being shunted from show to show. Adele Astaire introduced it in the Philadelphia tryout of 1924's *Lady, Be Good!*, but it was dropped before the Broadway opening. In 1927 it was matched with a male version, titled "The Girl I Love," and put into the original production of *Strike Up the Band*, which closed before reaching New York. Next, it was given to Marilyn Miller to sing in 1928's *Rosalie* and again it got dropped. Nonetheless, the song was taken up by Helen Morgan and other torch singers and became a hit on radio and in recordings and sheet music sales.

**from *Strike Up the Band***  Words by Ira Gershwin; Music by George Gershwin

# LOOKING FOR A BOY

The Florida land boom of the mid-1920s inspired two 1925 Broadway musical comedies with Florida settings: Irving Berlin's *Cocoanuts* (with the Marx Brothers) and the Gershwins' *Tip-Toes* (with Queenie Smith and, in a small role, Jeanette MacDonald). Not only was *Cocoanuts* the bigger hit, but George Gershwin saw his *Tip-Toes* score upstaged by his own *Piano Concerto in F*, which was premiered by the New York Philharmonic the same month. Still, some critics compared *Tip-Toes'* score favorably with the intimacy of Jerome Kern's Princess Theatre shows, such as *Very Good Eddie, Oh Boy!, Oh, Lady! Lady!!* and *Leave It to Jane.* Gershwin biographer Ed Jablonski has called "Looking for a Boy," in particular, a "tribute to Kern with Gershwin overtones — a bittersweet blue note, the rich harmonies, the engaging lilt of the melody."

from *Tip-Toes*
Words by Ira Gershwin; Music by George Gershwin

194   *Smaller hands can play:

# I GOTTA RIGHT TO SING THE BLUES

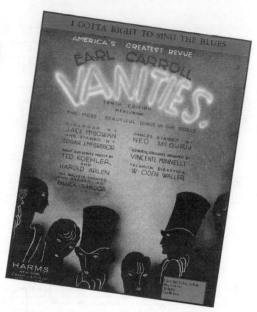

Earl Carroll was a major rival to Florenz Ziegfeld as a producer of lavish musical revues throughout the 1920s and early '30s. Over his stage door a sign proclaimed: "Through These Portals Pass the Most Beautiful Girls in the World." While working on Carroll's 1932 *Vanities*, Harold Arlen met one teenage chorine he considered the most beautiful of all, Anya Taranda. They were married several years later (and remained so until her death in 1970). The '32 *Vanities* also produced a lasting song hit for Arlen with "I Gotta Right to Sing the Blues." It may not have reflected his romantic state at the time, but it did catch the mood of many others during that Depression period. Louis Armstrong, Cab Calloway, and later Judy Garland all made memorable recordings of it.

**from *Earl Carroll's Vanities***     Words by Ted Koehler; Music by Harold Arlen

# COME RAIN OR COME SHINE

Among the white composers of the Broadway musical's Golden Age, Harold Arlen had the most intuitive feeling for black music, especially the blues. So he was a natural for the score of *St. Louis Woman*, the all-black 1946 musical starring Pearl Bailey and the Nicholas Brothers. Mixed reviews for the show's book, compounded by the economic jitters of that first post-war year, resulted in *St. Louis Woman* closing after 113 performances. Yet the bluesy "Come Rain or Come Shine" went on to three weeks on *Your Hit Parade* and has survived as a standard. Margaret Whiting, Jo Stafford, Judy Garland and Frank Sinatra are among the many who have recorded it.

**from *St. Louis Woman***     Words by Johnny Mercer; Music by Harold Arlen

I'm gon-na love you like no-bod-y's loved you come rain or come shine;___

High as a moun-tain and deep as a riv-er come

# BETWEEN THE DEVIL AND THE DEEP BLUE SEA

In the 1920s and early '30s, the revues at Harlem's famous Cotton Club rivaled those on Broadway in quality and popularity—with many Cotton Club songs quickly being picked up by radio and vaudeville performers. Singer Aida Ward and singer-dancer Bill ("Bojangles") Robinson introduced "Between the Devil and the Deep Blue Sea" in 1931's *Rhythmania*, the first Cotton Club revue for which Harold Arlen (then 26) provided the entire score. Over a four-year period, Arlen, mostly with Ted Koehler as lyricist, wrote some 35 songs for the shows, for which he received (according to biographer Ed Jablonski) $50 a week plus all the steak sandwiches he could eat. Presumably his royalties from this song provided lots more than sandwiches later on.

**Moderate bounce**

**from *Rhythmania***    Words by Ted Koehler; Music by Harold Arlen

*C10 = an open interval of a 10th, not really a chord.

# I'VE GOT THE WORLD ON A STRING

Another of the songs that Harold Arlen wrote in the early '30s for a Cotton Club revue, "I've Got the World on a String" was introduced by Aida Ward in the October 1932 edition of the string of revues called *Cotton Club Parade*. Its jaunty melody and happy-go-lucky lyrics quickly caught on with other singers seeking gloom-chasing tunes in those Depression years. A recording by the hottest young crooner of the day, Bing Crosby, turned it into a giant hit early in 1933. It has remained a pop standard ever since.

**from *Cotton Club Parade***  Words by Ted Koehler; Music by Harold Arlen

*Small notes are for more limited voices.

Life is a beau-ti-ful thing____ as long as I hold the string.____ I'd be a sil-ly so-and-so if I should ev-er let go.____ I've got the world on a string, sit-tin' on a rain-bow, got the string a-round my fin - ger. What a world! What a____ life! I'm in love.____

# HIT SONGS FROM HIT SHOWS OF THE '50s

# WHATEVER LOLA WANTS

## (LOLA GETS)

*Damn Yankees* (1955) is one of the few Broadway musicals to be made into a major film with its original star instead of with a replacement that Hollywood thought might be a stronger movie attraction. And so Gwen Verdon's inimitable performance as Lola, a temptress in the Devil's employ, is happily preserved for the ages. Verdon was in her element as both a dancer and comedy actress in this show, which combined elements of the classic Faust legend with a contemporary baseball story. When the Devil orders Lola to seduce the star pitcher, she assures him that "Whatever Lola wants, Lola gets!" Both Lola and the pitcher get more than they bargained for, and so too does the Devil. And Sarah Vaughan and Dinah Shore got hit recordings of the song.

**from *Damn Yankees***    Words and Music by Richard Adler and Jerry Ross

What happens when two sophisticated New Yorkers (the "fancy") mix with an isolated Amish community (the "plain") in rural Pennsylvania? Culture shock is the inevitable result—at least in the Broadway musical *Plain and Fancy*, a major success of the 1955 season. Its big song hit was "Young and Foolish," in which the show's Amish hero (David Daniels) recalls the "young and foolish" romantic promises he made to his childhood sweetheart (Gloria Marlowe) and wishes that he could be young and foolish once again.

**from *Plain and Fancy***     Words by Arnold B. Horwitt; Music by Albert Hague

# IF I WERE A BELL

It's doubtful that the gamblers, bookies and struggling show-biz hopefuls of New York City were ever as lovably comical or as simple-heartedly colorful as Damon Runyon depicted them in his popular short stories—or as they appear in *Guys and Dolls*, the musical adapted from one of those tales, "The Idyll of Sarah Brown." But it takes no suspension of belief to recognize *Guys and Dolls* as one of the all-time great musical comedies of the American theater. Its original Broadway production appeared in 1950, and several smash-hit revivals have followed, including the Tony-winning one of 1992. "If I Were a Bell" is one of Frank Loesser's right-on-target romantic tunes, summing up exactly how many of us feel when we realize we're in love.

**from *Guys and Dolls***     Words and Music by Frank Loesser

Ask me how do I feel, ask me now that we're co-zy and cling - ing.
(Ask me) how do I feel, from this chem-is - try les-son I'm learn - ing.

Well, sir, all I can say is if I were a bell I'd be
Well, sir, all I can say is if I were a bridge I'd be

# DIAMONDS ARE A GIRL'S BEST FRIEND

No musical comedy has portrayed the flappers and gold diggers of the 1920s more endearingly (and enduringly) than Anita Loos's *Gentlemen Prefer Blondes*. Originally a serial feature in *Harper's Bazaar* magazine, Loos's account of two young women's adventures trying to snare rich men captured the public fancy in the mid-'20s to such a degree that Loos published the collection as a book, then turned it into a hit Broadway play. Two decades later, in 1949, she helped transform it into an even bigger hit musical. Night after night, Carol Channing stopped the show singing "Diamonds Are a Girl's Best Friend," the impudently tongue-in-cheek gold-digger song. (All five verses are included here.) Marilyn Monroe sang the song in the 1953 movie version.

**from *Gentlemen Prefer Blondes***   Words by Leo Robin; Music by Jule Styne

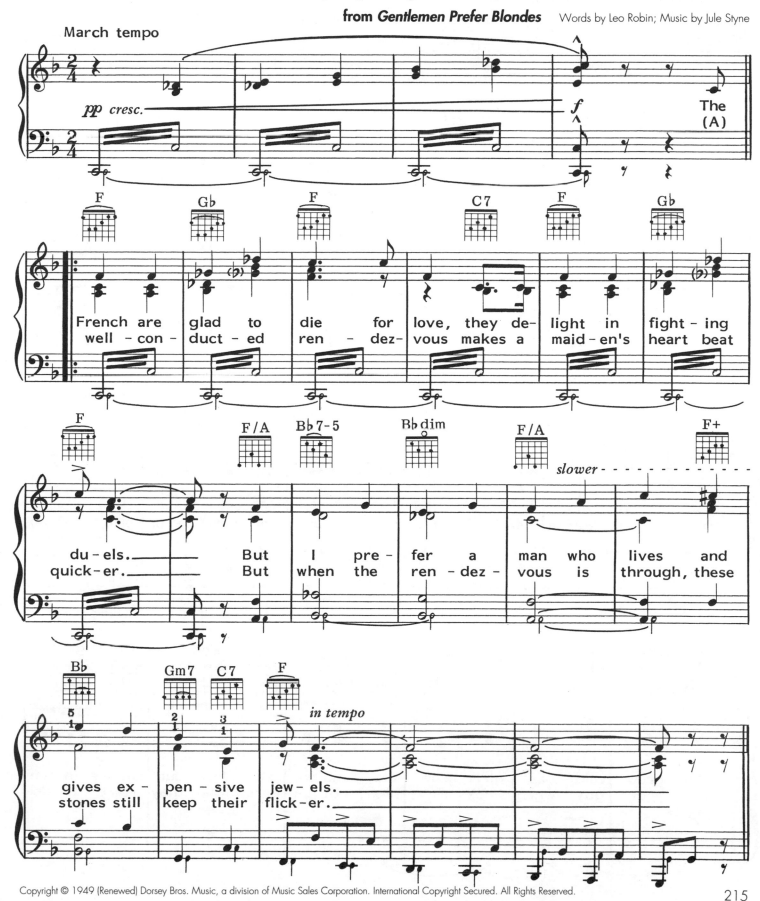

*(Additional lyrics from the original stage production)*

Romance is divine, and I'm not one to knock it,
But diamonds are a girl's best friend.
Romance is divine, yes, but where can you hock it?
When the flame is gone,
Just try and pawn a tired Don Juan.
Some men buy and some just sigh
That to make you their bride they intend.
But buyers or sighers
They're such g--d--- liars!
Diamonds are a girl's best friend.

I've heard of affairs that are strictly platonic,
But diamonds are a girl's best friend.
And I think affairs that you must keep Masonic
Are better bets
If little pets get big baguettes.
Time rolls on, and youth is gone,
And you can't straighten up when you bend.
But stiff back or stiff knees
You stand straight at Tiff-ny's!
Diamonds are a girl's best friend.

At Yale there's a lad whose appeal I acknowledge,
But diamonds are a girl's best friend.
I might like his dad but when I meet a college boy
The thing I say is 'ray, 'ray, 'ray for Cartier!
Some girls find
Some peace of mind
In a trust fund that banks recommend.
But if you are busty
Your trustee gets lusty!
Diamonds are a girl's best friend.

*(from the 𝄋 sign)*

Stash those rocks in your strongbox
For on them you can always depend.
It's not compensation, it's self-preservation!
Diamonds are a girl's best friend
(I don't **mean** rhinestones),
Diamonds are a girl's best friend.

# I'VE GROWN ACCUSTOMED TO HER FACE

Drama critic Brooks Atkinson once called George Bernard Shaw "a puritanical intellectual who despised the mating routines of the popular theater." How, then, in converting Shaw's *Pygmalion* into the 1956 musical *My Fair Lady,* could the proper, somewhat icy Professor Higgins (Rex Harrison) be shown to have fallen in love with Liza (Julie Andrews)? Songwriters Lerner and Loewe came up with the perfect solution at the end of the show with "I've Grown Accustomed to Her Face," tailored especially to Harrison's limited singing range. The song's lyrics not only move the show to a fittingly romantic conclusion but also express the sentiments of millions of other non-Shavian mortals.

**from *My Fair Lady***     Words by Alan Jay Lerner; Music by Frederick Loewe

# Love Is a Simple Thing

The various *New Faces* revues from the 1930s to the '60s introduced such notable talents to Broadway as Imogene Coca, Eve Arden, Henry Fonda, Van Johnson, Paul Lynde, Eartha Kitt, Madeline Kahn and Maggie Smith. Yet none of the series' many songs has proved as durable as the '52 edition's "Love Is a Simple Thing." Love, of course, has been described in song in many ways—from the sweetest thing to a many-splendored thing to something that's sweeping the country. But June Carroll and Arthur Siegel put it most succinctly and, yes, *simply.* Singer-pianist Siegel, however, had second thoughts some years later and wrote a satiric sequel, "Love Is a Complicated Mess," for his own supper club act. We still prefer the original.

**from *New Faces of 1952***     Words by June Carroll; Music by Arthur Siegel

221

# I'LL BUY YOU A STAR

The 1951 musical version of *A Tree Grows in Brooklyn,* based on Betty Smith's best-selling novel and the popular 1945 film, marked a significant departure for composer Arthur Schwartz. Up to then he had been identified largely with smart, sophisticated, contemporary shows such as *Between the Devil* and *The Band Wagon*—far cries from the nostalgic sentimentality and earthiness of Smith's tale of a Brooklyn tenement family in the early 1900s. But Schwartz produced, as Broadway historian Stanley Green noted, "a score that caught all the poignance and emotion of the gallant Nolan family." That's particularly true with "I'll Buy You a Star," in which the ne'er-do-well Johnny Nolan tries to reassure his hardworking wife Katie about their future.

**from *A Tree Grows in Brooklyn***     Words by Dorothy Fields; Music by Arthur Schwartz

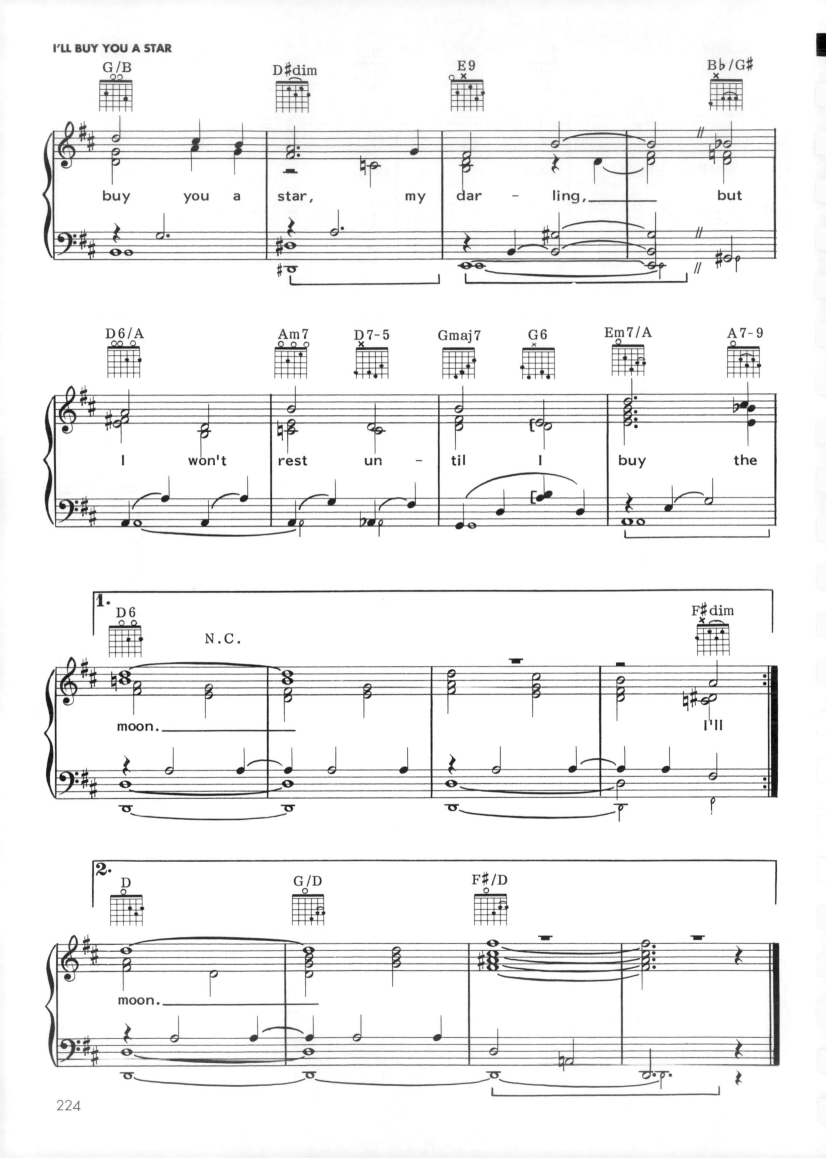

Two of Broadway's biggest musical hits of the late '50s each had leading characters named Maria—and each also had a song with her name as its title. In Rodgers and Hammerstein's 1959 *The Sound of Music,* the nuns of a Salzburg abbey sing about their most problematic postulant in the Act I song "Maria." Two years earlier, in *West Side Story's* "Maria," the young Polish-American Tony (Larry Kert) pours out his heart in song about the Puerto Rican girl (Carol Lawrence) he's just met and fallen in love with. Stephen Sondheim and Leonard Bernstein's romantic song is the one that the public took to *its* heart, with big boosts from popular recordings by Johnny Mathis and Andy Williams.

**from *West Side Story***    Words by Stephen Sondheim; Music by Leonard Bernstein

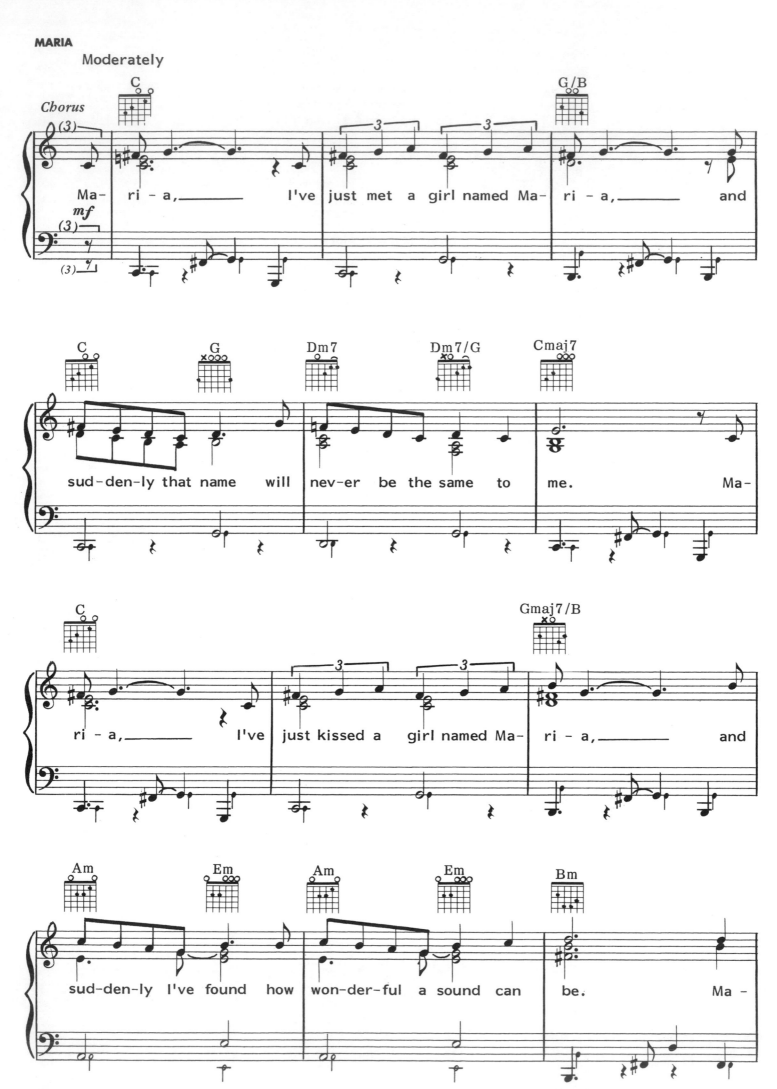

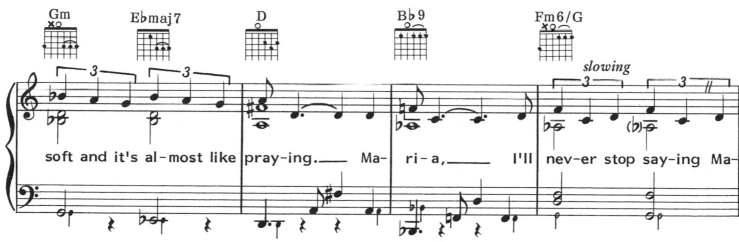

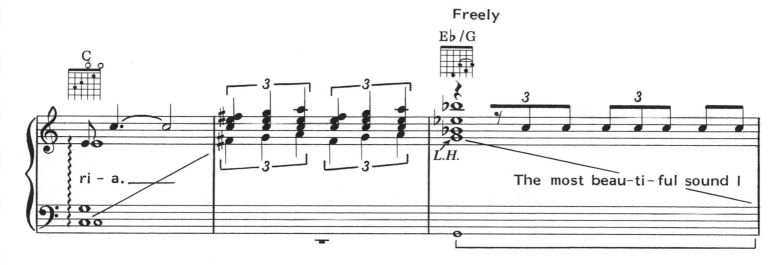

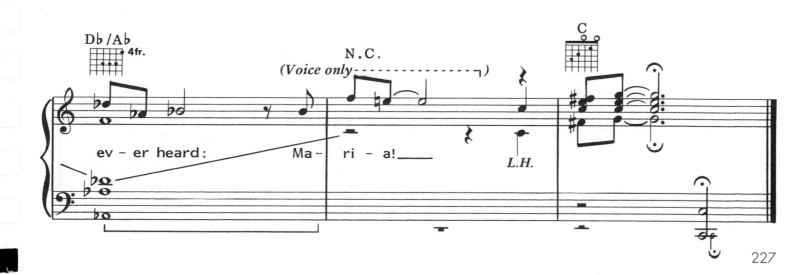

227

# THE PARTY'S OVER

*Bells Are Ringing*, in 1956, was Judy Holliday's first Broadway musical. It came 10 years after she achieved stardom in the comedy *Born Yesterday* and six years after she won an Oscar for the film version of that show. But Judy wasn't a musical newcomer when she sang in *Bells*. Early in her career she had been part of a New York club act called The Revuers, together with Betty Comden, Adolph Green and a young pianist billed as Lenny Amber (who stuck with his real name, Leonard Bernstein, for concert engagements). In *Bells Are Ringing*, Holliday sang the wistful "The Party's Over" when, at a glittering party, everything seems (wrongly, it turns out) to have ruined her chances of winning the show's leading man. Moral: The party's never really over even when you sing about it.

**from *Bells Are Ringing***      Words by Betty Comden and Adolph Green; Music by Jule Styne

flick - er and dim.___ You danced and dreamed through the night, it seemed to be right just be - ing with him.___ Now you must wake up,___ all dreams must end.___ Take off your make-up; The par-ty's o - ver,___ it's all o - ver,___ my friend.___ The par-ty's friend.

# LONG-RUNNING HITS FROM THE '60s

# SUNRISE, SUNSET

The unbelievable speed with which the years seem to pass and children grow has never been as touchingly set to music as in "Sunrise, Sunset." It's sung in *Fiddler on the Roof* by the Jewish dairyman Tevye and his wife, Golde, at the wedding of their eldest daughter in their impoverished village in czarist Russia. Instants later, the wedding is interrupted by a violent attack on the region's Jews by the Czar's police. The alternately heartwarmingly comic and heartbreakingly tragic *Fiddler* is based on a story by Sholom Aleichem. Zero Mostel created Tevye for Broadway in 1964. He was followed by Herschel Bernardi, Luther Adler, Jan Peerce and Chaim Topol, among others. Topol also played the lead in the 1971 movie version.

**from *Fiddler on the Roof***      Words by Sheldon Harnick; Music by Jerry Bock

swift – ly___ fly the years;

One sea – son fol-low-ing an – oth – er,

la – den with hap-pi-ness and tears.

*held back*

**1.**

**2.**

tears.___ *very lightly*

The Pulitzer Prize-winning *How to Succeed in Business Without Really Trying* (1961) is one of the few Broadway musical comedies to be successfully based on a *nonfiction* bestseller. The source: Shepherd Mead's satirical guide to climbing the corporate ladder. With only the thinnest of plotlines, the musical traced the comic exploits of a baby-faced young man (Robert Morse) who worked his way up from window washer to the executive suite—*not* by old-fashioned hard work but by wily applications of Mead's guidebook. Skewered along the way: company yes-men, old-school ties, manipulative secretaries, office parties and lots more. The hero even sings the mock-heroic "I Believe in You" to his own image in the men's room mirror.

# I BELIEVE IN YOU

from *How to Succeed in Business Without Really Trying*

Words and Music by Frank Loesser

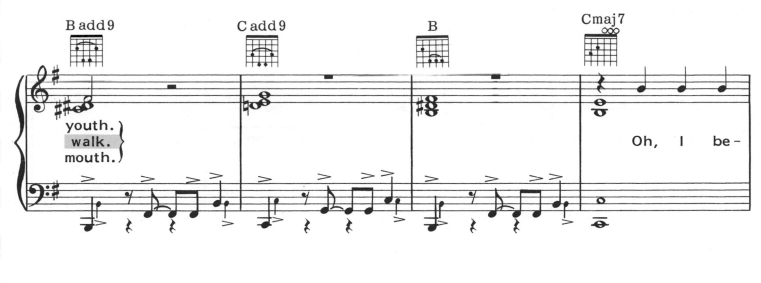

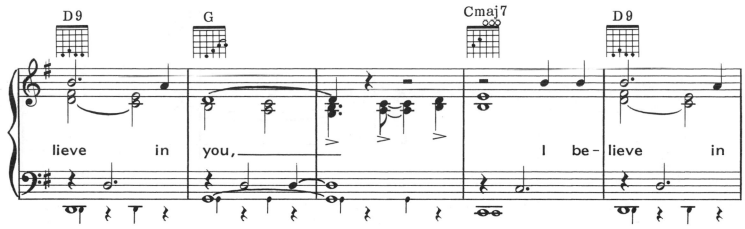

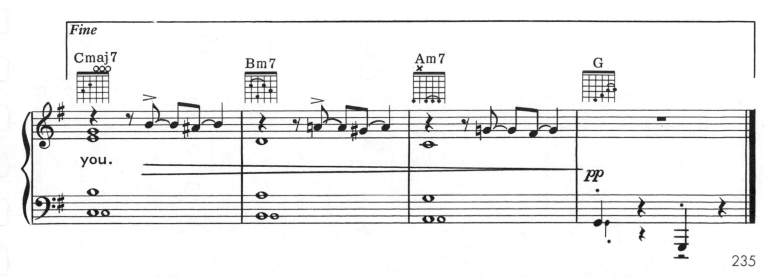

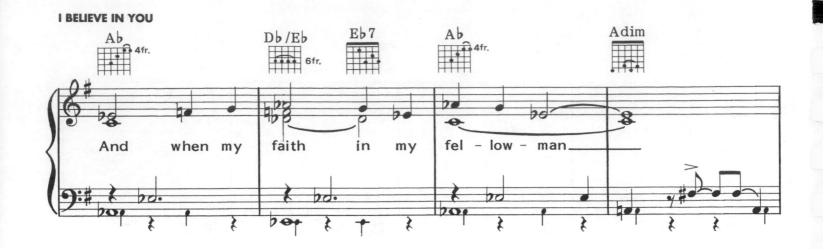

And when my faith in my fel – low – man

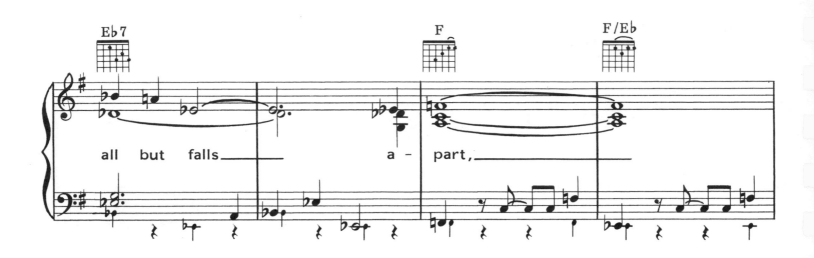

all but falls a – part,

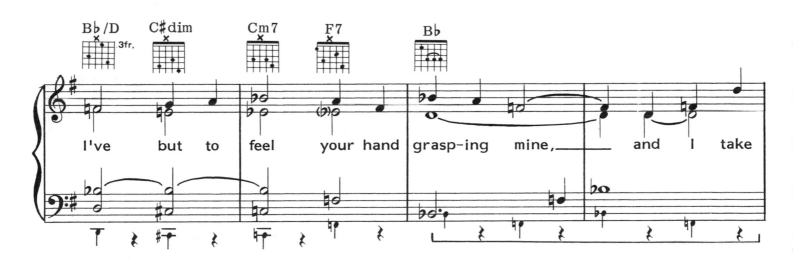

I've but to feel your hand grasp-ing mine, and I take

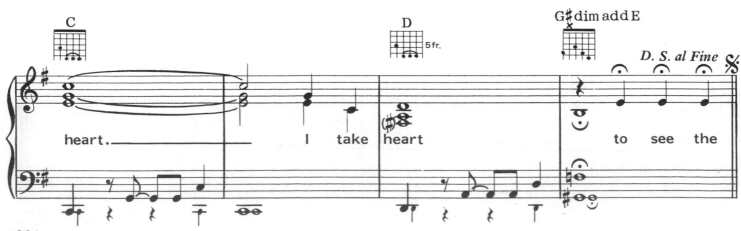

heart. I take heart to see the

*D. S. al Fine*

# HEY, LOOK ME OVER!

The multifaceted Cy Coleman (composer, jazz pianist, supper-club and concert-hall performer) has said that the hardest song he ever had to write was the opening number for TV superstar Lucille Ball in her 1960 Broadway debut, *Wildcat*. Finally, after two weeks, he and lyricist Carolyn Leigh decided to risk the simple, direct and perhaps even corny approach of "Hey, Look Me Over!" After all, they reasoned, that's what everyone in the audience would be doing on Lucy's entrance anyway. Not only did it work for the show, but the song became a hit in its own right.

**from *Wildcat***                    Words by Carolyn Leigh; Music by Cy Coleman

March tempo

Hey, look me o - ver, lend me an ear; Fresh out of clo - ver, mort-gaged up to here.__ But don't pass the plate, folks, don't pass the cup;__ I fig-ure when-ev-er you're down and out the on-ly way is

239

# WHAT KIND OF FOOL AM I?

Although there had, of course, been earlier musical imports from London, the 1962 hit *Stop the World* is often credited with launching the "British invasion" that dominated Broadway's musical stages for most of the '70s and '80s. It was also ahead of its time in dealing with that '80s phenomenon, the hell-bent drive of the "me" generation for personal power, money and success. Co-author Anthony Newley originated the leading role of the symbolic Littlechap in both London and New York. Each night he ended the show with "What Kind of Fool Am I?," Littlechap's dramatic facing-up to the empty spoils of his misdirected life. The song was on *Your Hit Parade* for 17 weeks.

from *Stop the World—I Want to Get Off*          Words and Music by Leslie Bricusse and Anthony Newley

# WALKING HAPPY

Songwriters Jimmy Van Heusen and Sammy Cahn are best known for the dozens of hit songs they wrote for movie musicals. On three occasions their joint efforts won them Academy Awards for Best Song, and each man (often working with other collaborators) holds a record for Oscar nominations. On Broadway they had less luck with two '60s musicals that enjoyed only modest runs, *Skyscraper* (1965) and *Walking Happy* (1966). The latter was based on the British play *Hobson's Choice*, best known to Americans for David Lean's 1953 film starring Charles Laughton and John Mills. The title song of the musical version achieved more popularity than either the show itself or its star, English comedian Norman Wisdom.

**from *Walking Happy***     Words by Sammy Cahn; Music by James Van Heusen

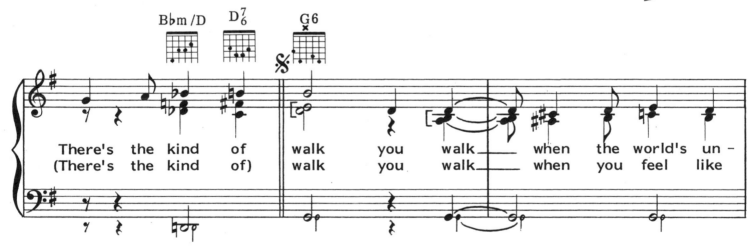

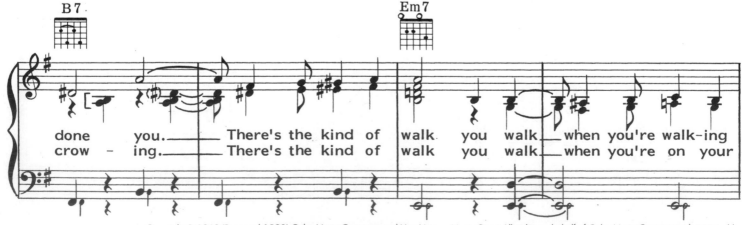

ver - y much like walk - ing on a cloud;
your heart's hop - pin' like a pop - in -

Good for - tune found you, chap - pie, and your life's a

hap - py val - en - tine._____ When you're walk - ing hap - py,

don't the bloom - in' world seem fine? There's the kind of

244

jay. So you had best be - lieve it, chap-pie.

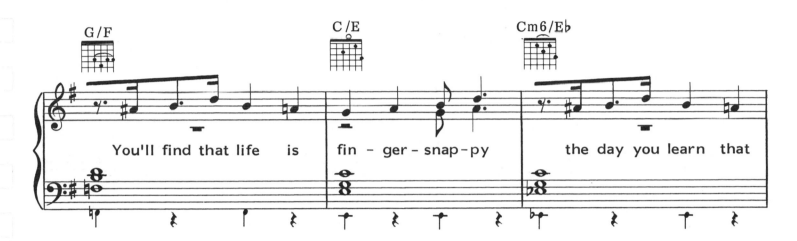

You'll find that life is fin - ger - snap-py the day you learn that

walk-ing hap-py gives the world a shine. So

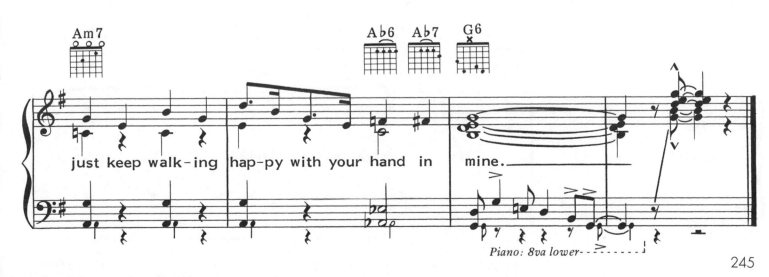

just keep walk-ing hap-py with your hand in mine.

*Piano: 8va lower- - - - - - - - - -*

# IF HE WALKED INTO MY LIFE

After the book, play and movie *Auntie Mame* turned Patrick Dennis's free-spirited title character into everyone's favorite "dream aunt," a musical version of her adventures seemed inevitable. Jerry Herman obliged with his *Mame*, in 1966. His songs gave additional depth and even pathos to Mame's screwball character, particularly with "If He Walked Into My Life," in which Mame looks back over the years and examines how she raised her orphaned nephew. *Mame* made a Broadway superstar of Angela Lansbury, who lost the role in the 1974 movie version to another superstar, Lucille Ball. Meanwhile, a recording by Eydie Gorme gave the lyrics of "If He Walked Into My Life" a broader romantic skew and turned the song into a hit.

**from *Mame***    Words and Music by Jerry Herman

Slowly

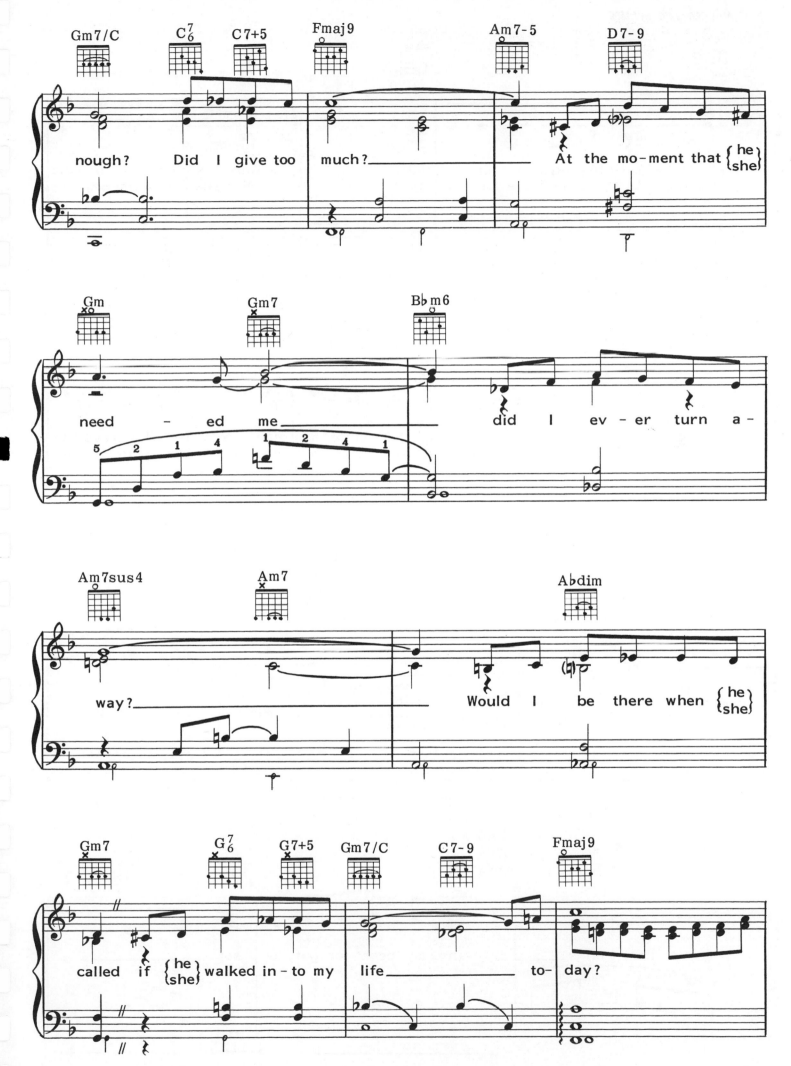

Female Version: Were his days a lit-tle dull? Were his nights a lit-tle
Male Version: Did she mind the lone-ly nights? Did she count the emp-ty

wild? Did I o-ver-state my plan? Did I stress the
days? Was I si-lent? Was I cold? Was I quick to

man and for-get the child? And there must have been a
scold? Was I slow to praise?

mil - lion things that my heart for-got to say.

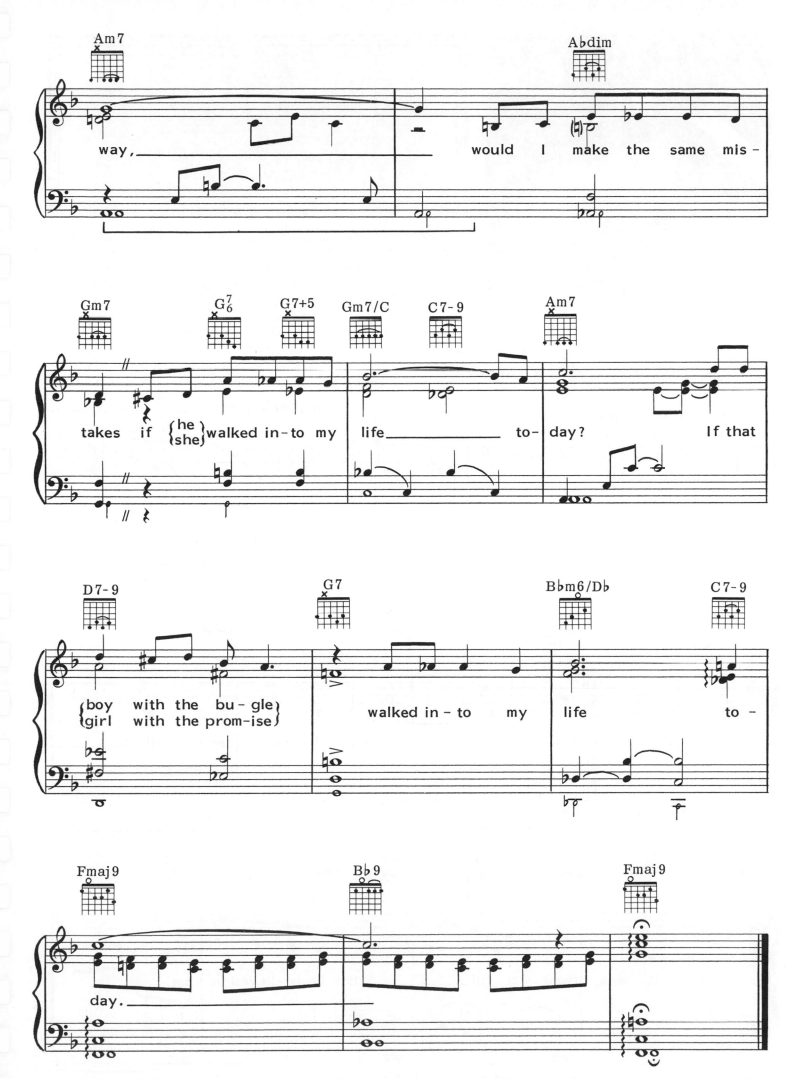

# AND I WAS BEAUTIFUL

Jerry Herman took the old saying "Beauty is in the eye of the beholder" and spun it around for this song's lyrics—to reflect the beholder's view *back* to the leading character of *Dear World*. Played on Broadway by Angela Lansbury, she's an aging, eccentric Parisian countess whose looks faded years ago. Yet she sings about how the forsaken lover of her youth could make her feel beautiful with just a glance, and how the memory of that glance can still work its magic. *Dear World* was adapted from French playwright Jean Giraudoux's allegorical comedy *The Madwoman of Chaillot*. In it, the countess and her cronies battle the greedy industrialists who want to drill for oil beneath the streets of Paris.

**from *Dear World***    Words and Music by Jerry Herman

**Slowly, with feeling**

He stood and looked at me ___ and I was beau - ti - ful, ___ for it was beau - ti - ful ___ how he be - lieved in me.

# SOON IT'S GONNA RAIN

The weather forecast in *The Fantasticks* brought much more than the proverbial raining of "pennies from heaven" to its box office. A downpour of success turned this Off-Broadway musical into the longest-running stage production in New York history. In fact, in 1993, as this songbook goes to press, *The Fantasticks* is still playing at the same theater in New York's Greenwich Village in which it opened in 1960. Adapted from *Les Romanesques*, an 1894 French play by Edmond Rostand (author of *Cyrano de Bergerac*), *The Fantasticks* is an eight-character fable about young love and family relationships. In this song the young lovers vow to keep both real and metaphorical storms from separating them.

**from *The Fantasticks***   *Words by Tom Jones; Music by Harvey Schmidt*

# BIG SPENDER

Although it was long commonplace for Broadway plays to be turned into movies, until the 1960s it was rare for the reverse to occur, especially for a serious film to be transformed into a Broadway musical. *Sweet Charity* made such a transition by changing the locale of Federico Fellini's Oscar-winning Italian film *The Nights of Cabiria* from Rome to New York and by turning its leading character, a romantically naive prostitute, into a taxi dancer. The show's sardonic "Big Spender" makes it clear exactly what the lady and her dance-hall colleagues are all about. Gwen Verdon played Charity in Bob Fosse's original 1966 production; Shirley MacLaine had the role in the 1969 movie version.

**from *Sweet Charity***   Words by Dorothy Fields; Music by Cy Coleman

Moderately, with a beat

*snap fingers*

The min-ute you walked in the joint I could see you were a

man of dis-tinc-tion, a real big spend-er, good look-ing, so re-fined.__ Say,

would-n't you like to know what's go-ing on in my mind?__ So let me get

right to the point: I don't pop my cork for ev-'ry guy I see.

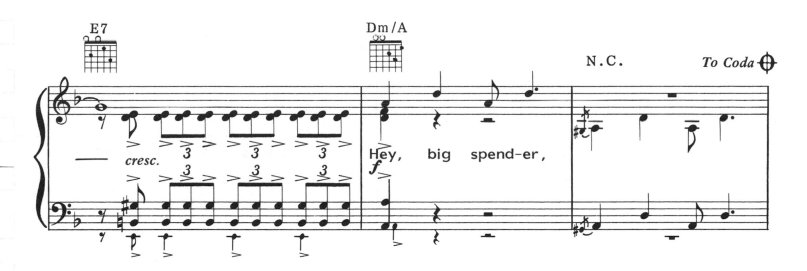

cresc. Hey, big spend-er,

N.C.    To Coda ✛

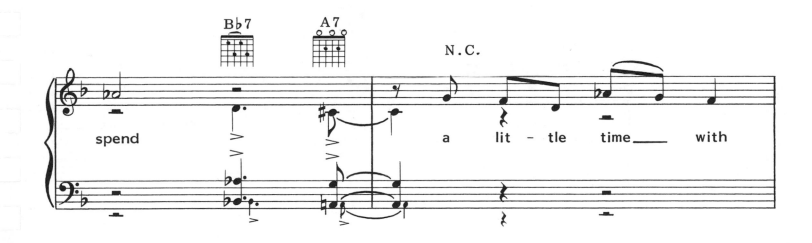

spend    a lit-tle time____ with

N.C.

me.

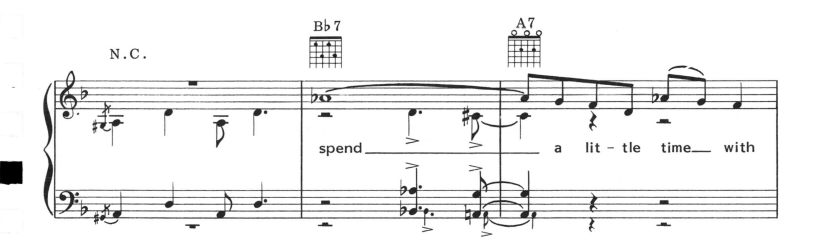

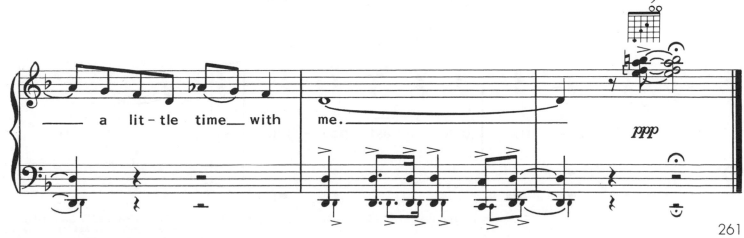

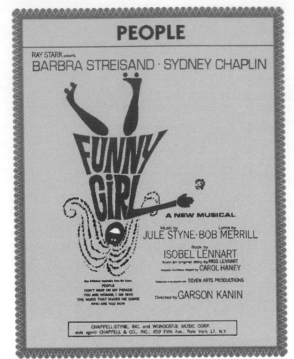

"People" is one of the few songs that became a hit *before* the opening of the Broadway show for which it was written. That's because *Funny Girl*, the story of singer-comedian Fanny Brice, endured several postponements before its March 1964 opening and four changes of directors (Jerome Robbins, Bob Fosse, Garson Kanin and then back to Robbins). Meanwhile, Barbra Streisand, little known outside New York when she was signed for the lead, began skyrocketing to national fame through recordings and television appearances. Four years after the Broadway opening, Streisand won a Best Actress Oscar for the movie version of *Funny Girl*.

**from Funny Girl**   Words by Bob Merrill; Music by Jule Styne

Moderately, with a Latin touch

Peo - ple, ___ peo - ple who need peo - ple ___ are the luck - i - est peo - ple ___ in the

265

# THE IMPOSSIBLE DREAM

Miguel de Cervantes' 16th-century novel of the knight Don Quixote has inspired several musical versions, including Reginald DeKoven's 1889 operetta, Richard Strauss's 1897 tone poem, Jules Massenet's 1910 opera *Don Quichotte* and the 1965 musical play *Man of La Mancha*. In the show's big hit, "The Impossible Dream," Don Quixote gives voice to his belief in the importance of striving to achieve the impossible even when it seems ridiculous—a credo refreshingly at odds with the despairing tone of many mid-'60s plays and movies. Richard Kiley, Jose Ferrer, Hal Holbrook, Keith Michell and Raul Julia are among those who have portrayed the Don on Broadway. Peter O'Toole played the role in the 1972 movie version.

**from *Man of La Mancha***      Words by Joe Darion; Music by Mitch Leigh

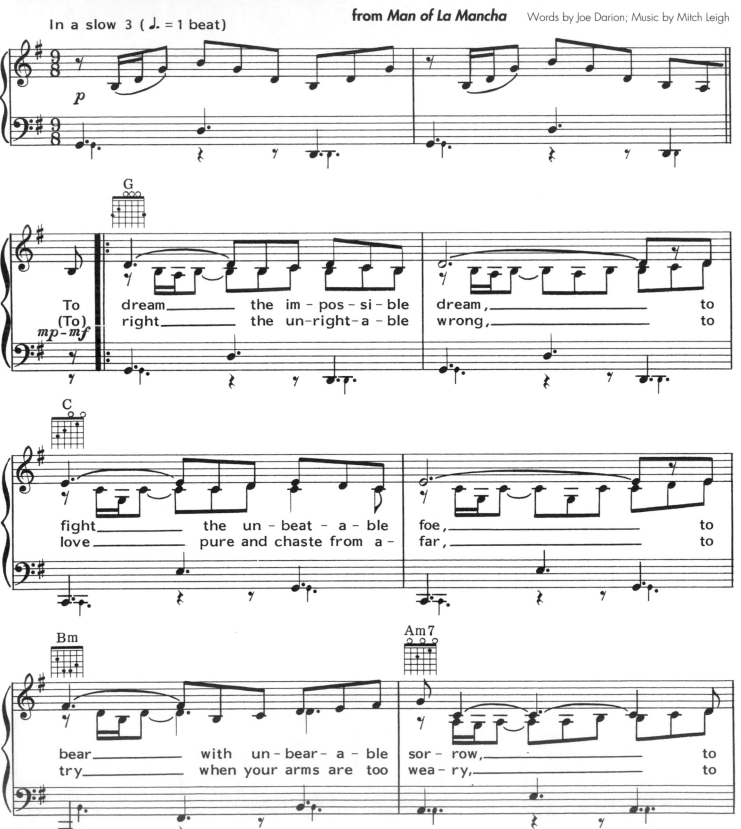

run_____ where the brave dare not go._____ To

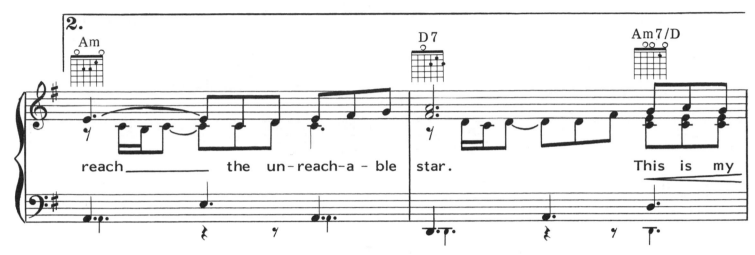

reach_____ the un-reach-a-ble star. This is my

quest:_____ To fol-low that star_____ no mat-ter how

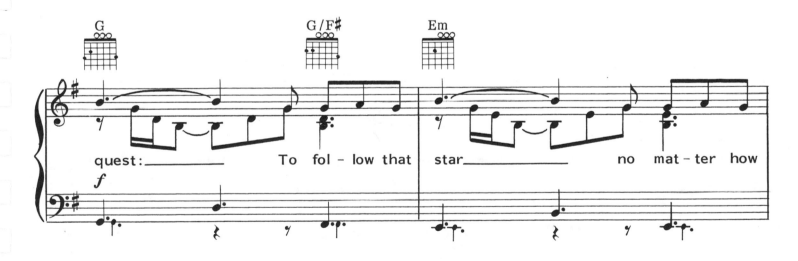

hope-less,_____ no mat-ter how far,_____ to fight for the

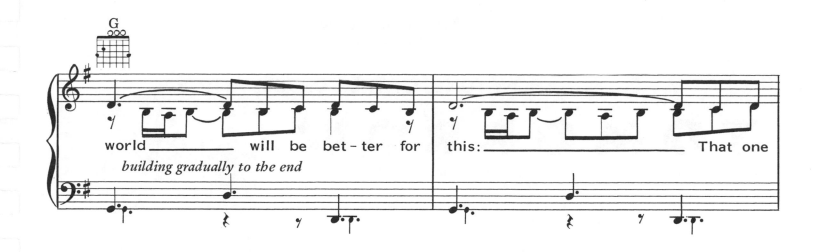

world _____ will be bet-ter for this: _____ That one

*building gradually to the end*

man, _____ scorned and cov-ered with scars, _____ still_____

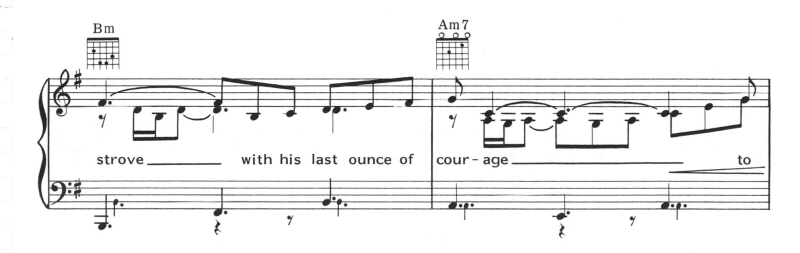

strove _____ with his last ounce of cour-age _____ to

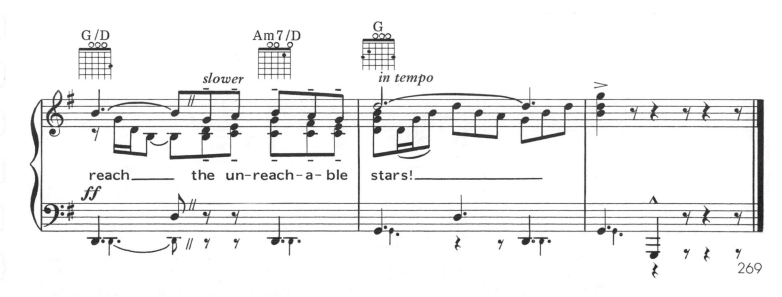

*slower*      *in tempo*

reach_____ the un-reach-a-ble stars! _____

*ff*

## A NEW ERA: SHOW TUNES OF THE '70s, '80s AND '90s

# TOMORROW

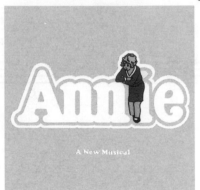

*Little Orphan Annie* has been a much-loved part of Americana since the 1920s—first as a comic strip, then as a radio serial, and finally as the Broadway musical hit *Annie*. The author of the musical's book, Thomas Meehan, saw the fictional waif as "a metaphorical figure standing for innate decency, courage, and optimism in the face of hard times, pessimism, and despair." Such qualities represented aspects of the Depression era in which *Annie* is set but they were also part of the Vietnam-Watergate period during which the show was written. By the time *Annie* opened on Broadway in 1977 (after a production the previous summer at the Goodspeed Opera in Connecticut), the national mood was more upbeat. Yet *Annie*'s sentimental charm and spunk still hit a responsive chord with theatergoers, especially when Annie sang the cheerfully optimistic "Tomorrow."

**Slowly, in 2 (♩ = 1 beat)**     **from *Annie***     Words by Martin Charnin; Music by Charles Strouse

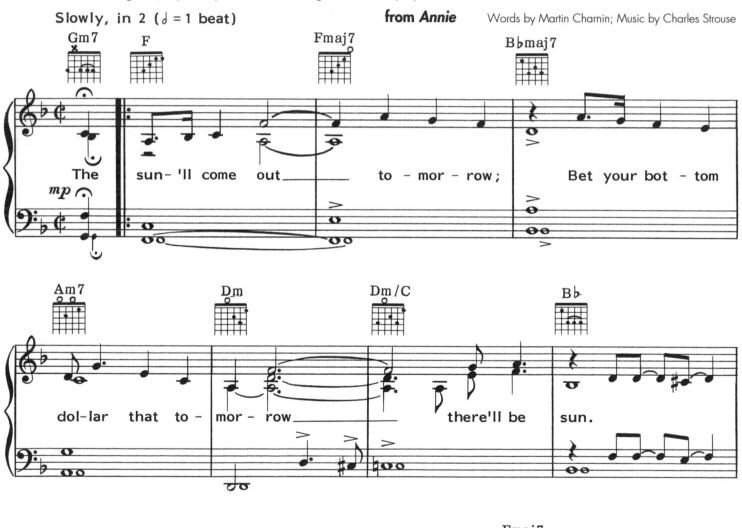

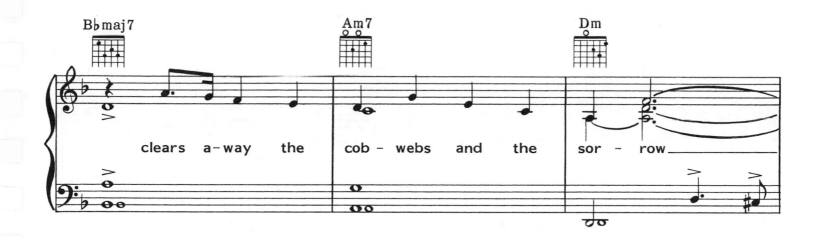

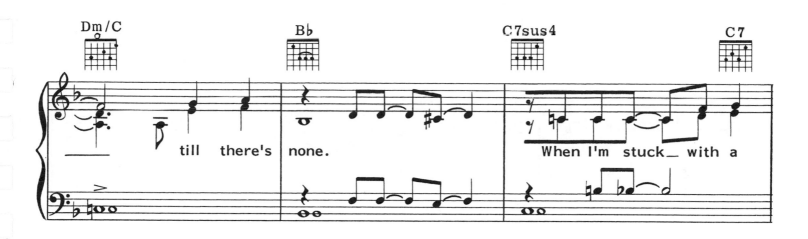

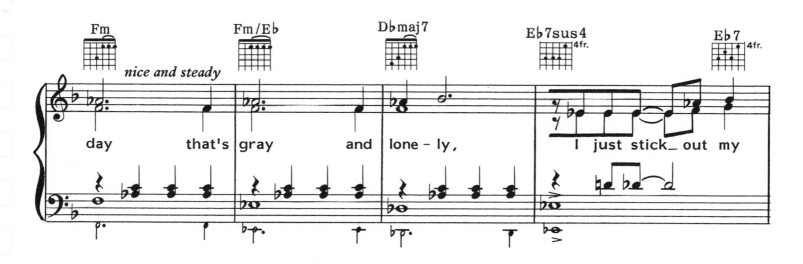

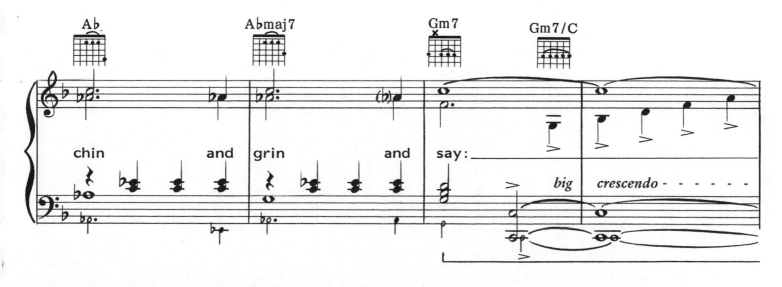

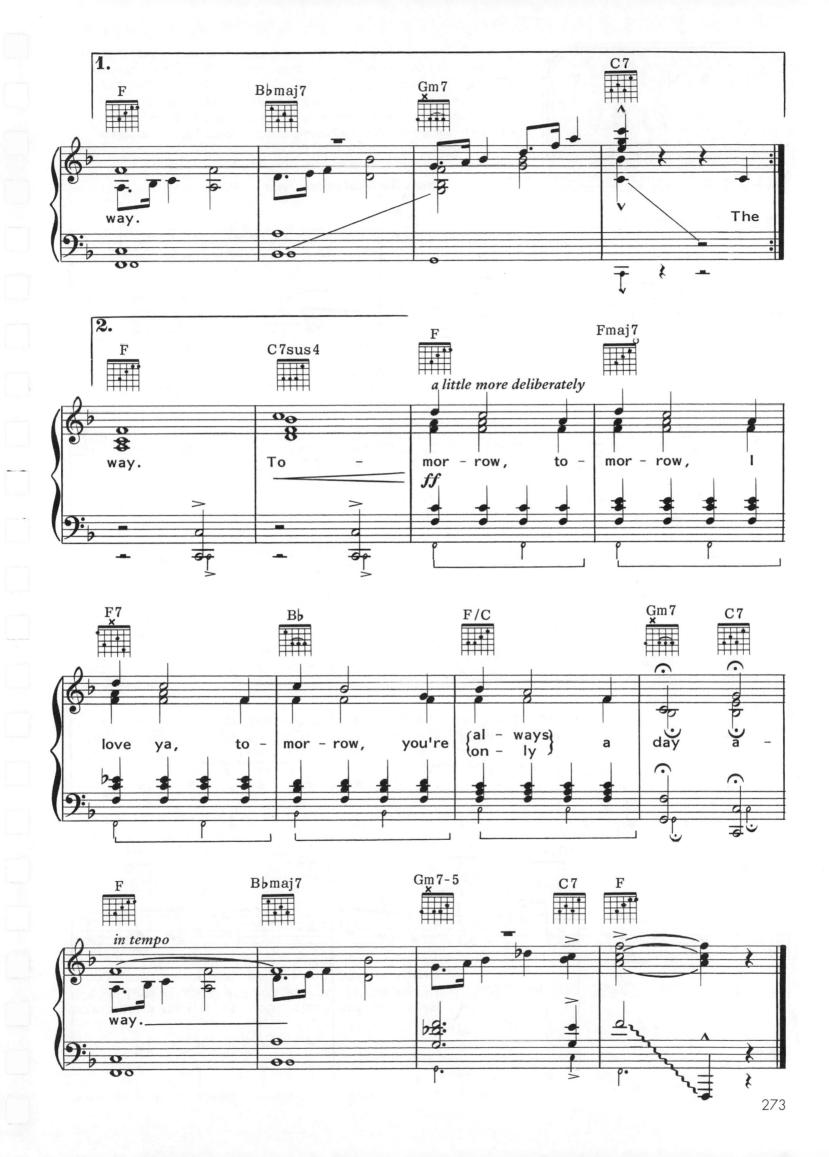

# STANDING ON THE CORNER

*Guys and Dolls* may be Frank Loesser's most popular musical, but there are many who consider *The Most Happy Fella* his finest. Adapted from Sidney Howard's 1925 Pulitzer Prize-winning play *They Knew What They Wanted*, *The Most Happy Fella* tells the story of Tony, an aging Italian-American grape grower in California, who woos a mail-order bride by sending her a photo of his ranch's handsome foreman—with inevitable complications. "Standing on the Corner" remains the show's most popular song. A 1991 revival of *The Most Happy Fella* featured Spiro Malas as Tony, a role first played by Robert Weede.

**from *The Most Happy Fella***          Words and Music by Frank Loesser

Interlude

Few contemporary comedies have enjoyed the international success of the 1978 film *La Cage aux Folles*, a French-Italian coproduction adapted from a hit Parisian play by Jean Poiret. It led not only to two movie sequels, but also to the 1983 Broadway musical adaptation by Harvey Fierstein, Arthur Laurents and Jerry Herman. Essentially an old-fashioned French farce with some decidedly unorthodox variations, the Riviera-set story centers on the complications that arise when the owner of a gay nightclub must meet his son's very proper prospective in-laws—and the father's male lover decides to impersonate the absent mother. In "The Best of Times" the club's chorus of female impersonators challenge the old cliché about waiting for tomorrow to be a better day and urge, instead, that the present be lived to its fullest.

# THE BEST OF TIMES

**from *La Cage aux Folles***

Words and Music by Jerry Herman

Moderately, in 2 ( ♩ = 1 beat)

The best of times is now; What's left of sum-mer but a fad - ed rose. The best of times is now; As for to-mor-row, well, who knows, who knows, who knows? So

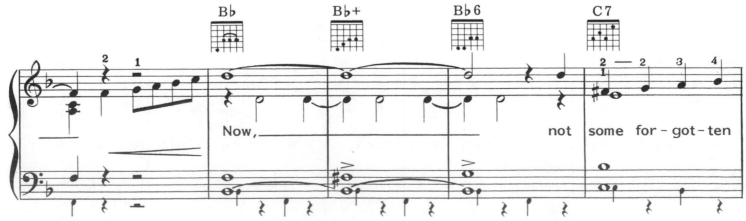

# ONE

A *Chorus Line* holds the record for being the longest-running musical ever to play a continuous engagement on Broadway—6,137 performances between 1975 and 1990. (*The Fantasticks* has run longer but it is technically an Off-Broadway production.) Arguably the showstopper to end all Broadway showstoppers, "One" is literally the song that ends the production—the number the entire show has been building toward and the number in which everything the auditioning dancers have been preparing finally comes together. As staged in the show, "One" is a glittering, exhilarating precision extravaganza, typical of Broadway-style song-and-dance routines for at least seven decades. It never failed to bring down the house during the show's record-breaking long run.

**from *A Chorus Line***     Words by Edward Kleban; Music by Marvin Hamlisch

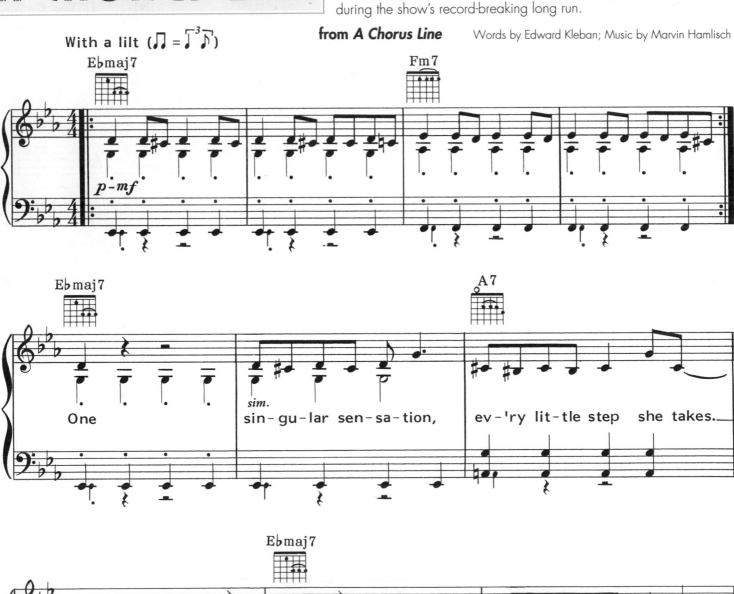

for the girl is sec-ond best ___ to none, son!

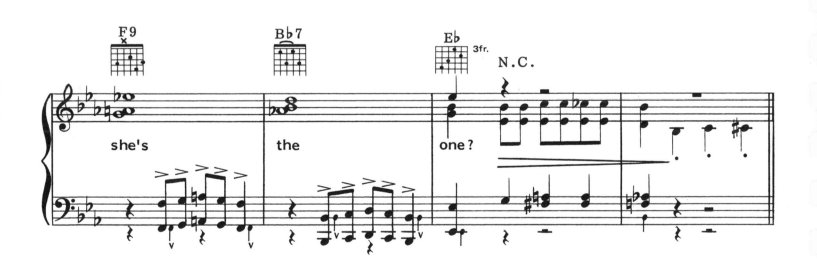

Ooh, sigh, give her your at-ten-tion. Do I real-ly have to men-tion

she's the one?

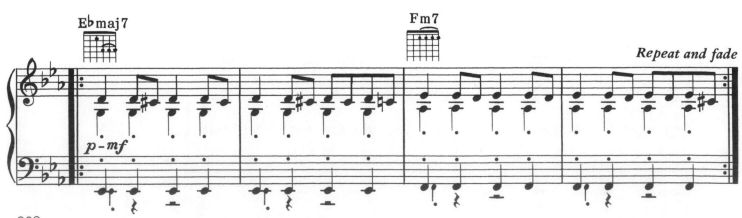

Repeat and fade

# YOU'RE GETTING TO BE A HABIT WITH ME

The usual Broadway-to-Hollywood progression did an about-face in 1980 when *42nd Street*, one of the best-known of all original movie musicals, was turned into a Broadway smash. Five of Harry Warren and Al Dubin's songs from the 1933 movie were retained (including "You're Getting to Be a Habit with Me"), and nine others by the same songwriters (from other '30s movies) were interpolated. "You're Getting to Be a Habit with Me" had earlier enjoyed a sort of double-entendre "comeback" relating to drugs in the '60s, but composer Warren always denied that neither lyricist Dubin's own drug problem (revealed after his death) or the underground drug culture among some musicians in the early '30s had inspired the song. Instead, he said, the idea came from a Warner Brothers secretary who remarked that she was uncertain about a guy she was going with, but that "he's getting to be a habit with me."

**from *42nd Street*** Words by Al Dubin; Music by Harry Warren

*Chorus*-Nice and perky

Ev-'ry kiss, ev-'ry hug seems to act just like a drug;__ You're get-ting to be a hab-it with me.__ Let me stay in your arms, I'm ad-dict-ed to your charms;__ You're get-ting to be a hab-it with me.__

# WHAT I DID FOR LOVE

The plotline for *A Chorus Line* involves an audition for dancers for a Broadway show and focuses on their individual dreams, stresses, fears, frustrations and joys as the audition proceeds. When one dancer is unexpectedly injured, the director asks the others what they'd do if they couldn't dance anymore. One replies with the song "What I Did for Love," in which she equates dancing with love and argues that it may be ended or lost but never forgotten. Priscilla Lopez introduced the song in the original production, in 1975.

**from *A Chorus Line***        Words by Edward Kleban; Music by Marvin Hamlisch

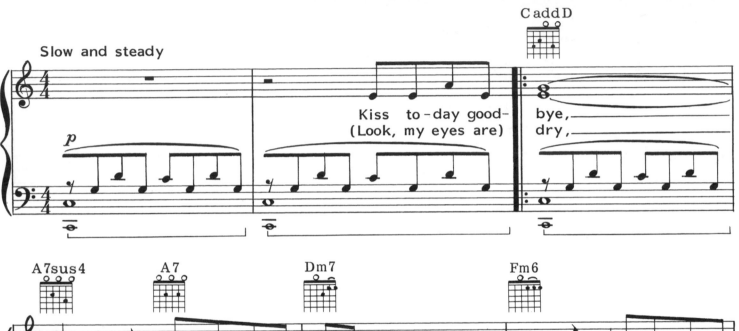

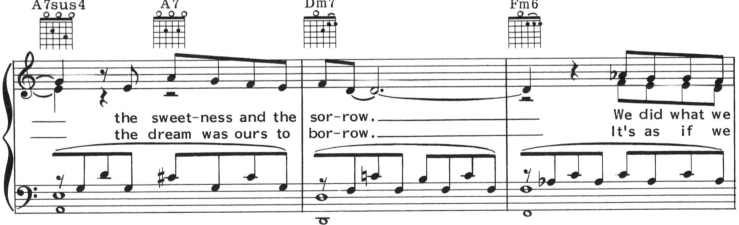